UNINTENDED

*How War in Iraq Strengthened
America's Enemies*

Simon & Schuster

CONSEQUENCES

Peter W. Galbraith

NEW YORK   LONDON   TORONTO   SYDNEY

Simon & Schuster
1230 Avenue of the Americas
New York, NY 10020

First Simon & Schuster hardcover edition September 2008

SIMON & SCHUSTER and colophon are registered trademarks of
Simon & Schuster, Inc.

For information about special discounts for bulk purchases,
please contact Simon & Schuster Special Sales at
1-800-456-6798 or business@simonandschuster.com

Designed by Nancy Singer

Manufactured in the United States of America

10   9   8   7   6   5   4   3   2   1

Library of Congress Cataloging-in-Publication Data
Galbraith, Peter (Peter W.)
   Unintended consequences: how war in Iraq strengthened America's
enemies / Peter W. Galbraith.
      p.   cm.
Includes bibliographical references and index.
   1. Iraq War, 2003–   2. Iraq—History—2003–   3. Iraq—History—
1991–2003.   4. United States—Military relations—Iraq.   5. Iraq—
Military Relations—United States.   6. Iraq—Ethnic relations.   I. Title.
DS79.76.G335   2008
956.7044'31—dc22   2008029889
ISBN-13: 978-1-4165-6225-2
ISBN-10:   1-4165-6225-7

For Nuala and Claiborne Pell
and
Elizabeth B. Moynihan
and in memory of
Daniel Patrick Moynihan.
And for Tone

The Moving Finger writes; and, having writ,
Moves on: nor all your Piety nor Wit
Shall lure it back to cancel half a Line,
Nor all your Tears wash out a Word of it.
                                —OMAR KHAYYAM

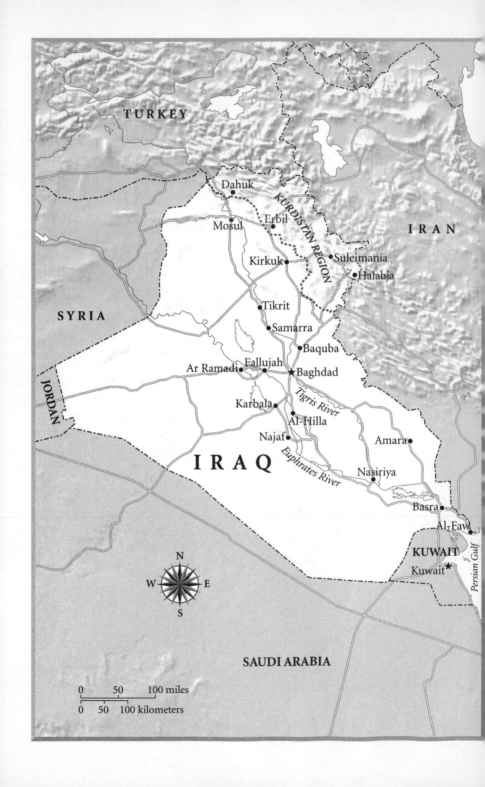

Iraq's Ethnic and Sectarian Divisions

Kurdistan: Situated in Iraq's northeast, the Kurdistan Region is a de facto independent state with its own president, parliament, flag, and army. Kurdistan's present boundaries follow the Green Line (shown as a dotted line on the map) that separated the Kurdish enclave established in 1991 from territory controlled by Saddam's army.

The Disputed Areas: Kirkuk and its surrounding governorate are at the heart of an eighty-year territorial dispute between Kurds and Arabs. The Kurds, who have controlled Kirkuk since helping liberate the province in 2003, want a referendum, as required by Iraq's Constitution, to determine whether Kirkuk is incorporated into Kurdistan. Kirkuk's Arabs and Turkmen oppose the referendum, which was postponed from its constitutionally required December 31, 2007, deadline. Kurds also claim a swath of territories south and west of the Green Line all the way from the Syrian border to the Iranian border. Arab Iraqis accept Kurdistan's annexation of much purely Kurdish inhabited territory but reject other of Kurdistan's claims.

The Sunni Center: Iraq's Sunni majority areas in Iraq's center and west form a rough triangle beginning at the tri-junction of Iraq, Jordan, and Saudi Arabia, going east to Baghdad's western suburbs and then heading northwest to Mosul and back southwest along the Syrian and Jordanian borders. The Sunni Center comprises: Anbar Governorate, which is 98 percent Sunni and includes the vast western desert bordering Saudi Arabia and Jordan and the one-time insurgent hotbeds of Fallujah and Ar Ramadi; Salahaddin Governorate, which includes Saddam Hussein's home region of Tikrit and Samarra, where the destruction of the Shiite Askariya shrine in February 2006 triggered a dramatic escalation of Iraq's Sunni-Shiite civil war; and most of Nineveh Governorate, with Mosul as its capital. Mosul, Iraq's third largest city, is divided by the Tigris River between a Sunni west and a Kurdish east. To Mosul's east are Christian villages that would like to form a majority Christian Nineveh Plain Autonomous Region; to the north, west, and east are Yazidi villages and towns; and to the west is volatile Tel Afar with its large Turkmen population.

The Shiite South: The southern half of Iraq is Shiite. This area is demarcated by a line starting on the Euphrates north of Karbala and extending east to the southern reaches of Baghdad and then on to the Iranian border. It includes the holy cities of Karbala and Najaf as well as Basra, Iraq's second city, and access to the Persian Gulf. Iraq's Council of Representatives has enacted a law permitting Iraq's nine southern Governorates to form a single Shiite Region with the same powers as Kurdistan.

Baghdad: Baghdad, with 20 percent of Iraq's population, is divided between a mostly Shiite east and a mostly Sunni west. After 2003, its once mixed neighborhoods became either Shiite or Sunni.

Contents

UNINTENDED CONSEQUENCES

Introduction

George W. Bush launched and lost America's Iraq War. Losing is just one way in which the Iraq War did not turn out as planned.

- A war intended to eliminate the threat from Saddam Hussein's nonexistent weapons of mass destruction ended up with Iran and North Korea much closer to having deployable nuclear weapons.
- A war intended to fight terror has helped the terrorists.
- A war intended to bring freedom and democracy to Iraq now has U.S. troops fighting for pro-Iranian Shiite theocrats and alongside unreformed Baathists.
- A war intended to undermine Iran's ayatollahs has resulted in a historic victory for Iran. Iranian-backed political parties control Iraq's government and armed forces, giving Iran a role in Iraq that it has not had in four centuries.
- A war intended to promoted democracy in the Middle East has set it back.

- A war intended to intimidate Syria and make Israel more secure has left Israel more threatened and Syria less isolated.
- A war intended to enhance America's relations with moderate Islam has made Turkey among the most anti-American countries in the world.
- A war intended to showcase American power has highlighted the deficiencies of U.S. intelligence, the incompetence of American administration, and the limitations on the American military.
- A war intended to boost American global leadership has driven U.S. prestige to an all-time low.
- A war intended to consolidate Republican power in Washington for a generation cost the GOP control of both houses of Congress in 2006, and seems likely to help elect an antiwar Democrat president in 2008.
- A war intended to make America more secure has left the country weaker.

"The United States of America will not permit the world's most dangerous regimes to threaten us with the world's most destructive weapons," President Bush told Congress in his first State of the Union speech, on January 29, 2002. America, he promised, will "deny terrorists and their state sponsors the materials, technology, and expertise to make and deliver weapons of mass destruction." And he warned, "America will do what is necessary to ensure our nation's security."

George W. Bush's performance never matched his rhetoric. A year after that speech, he launched a war to eliminate Iraqi weapons of mass destruction that did not exist. Meanwhile, North Korea—a country he said was in an "Axis of Evil" with Iraq and Iran—took advantage of Bush's preoccupation with a phantom Iraqi threat and withdrew from the Nuclear Non-Proliferation Treaty. North Korea went on to make eight nuclear weapons from plutonium that had previously been safeguarded by the International Atomic Energy Agency (IAEA) and then tested one in 2006. President Bush did nothing about North Korea for years before eventually concluding an agreement that required North Korea to dismantle its aging reactor but effectively allowed it to keep its nukes.

Iraq did not have a nuclear program but Iran does. From 1985 to 2003, Iran ran a clandestine program aimed at acquiring the technology to enrich uranium that could be used as the fissile material for a nuclear weapon. In 2003, Iran disclosed this clandestine program to the IAEA and agreed to freeze its uranium enrichment activities. George Bush's Iraq War paved the way for Iran's Shiite allies to take power in Iraq in 2005. With American troops bogged down in Iraq and its own strategic position incomparably stronger, Iran resumed enriching uranium in 2005 and has defied subsequent U.N. Security Council resolutions demanding that it stop. George Bush designated Iran part of the Axis of Evil in 2002 and accused those who want to negotiate with Iran of appeasement. This tough language is a diversion from the fact that George W. Bush has done nothing diplomatically, militarily, or otherwise to slow down Iran's nuclear program.

On George W. Bush's watch, Pakistan was the world's most dangerous nuclear proliferator. It provided nuclear weapons technology to North Korea, Iran, Libya, and, almost certainly, other states. Prior to the terrorist attacks of September 11, 2001, its nuclear scientists even met with al-Qaeda in Afghanistan. When its nuclear activities became public in 2004, George W. Bush meekly accepted the explanation of Pakistan's dictator,

Pervez Musharraf, that it was all a rogue operation run by Pakistani nuclear scientist A. Q. Khan. Bush never complained when Musharraf pardoned the supposed rogue a day after he confessed to running a proliferation ring or when Pakistan stonewalled U.S. requests to interview Khan.

George W. Bush did not keep his promise to "do what is necessary to ensure our nation's security." As an unintended consequence of his Iraq War, the countries of Iran, North Korea, and Pakistan all became more dangerous threats to America's security.

Saddam Hussein had no role in the 9/11 attacks, as everyone now agrees. President Bush, however, insists that the Iraq War is an integral part of the war on terror. He has a point. George W. Bush gave al-Qaeda its opening in Iraq. If Iraq is now the central front in the war on terror, it is because George W. Bush made it so.

Prior to the invasion of Iraq, al-Qaeda was not in any part of Iraq controlled by Saddam Hussein. Al-Qaeda saw Saddam Hussein as a corrupt secular nationalist, precisely the kind of Arab leader it wanted to depose.* Saddam Hussein had few virtues, but in this unique case the United States was well served by his ruthless approach to internal opponents.

On April 9, 2003, U.S. troops took Baghdad on the orders of a president whose administration had made no plans to provide security or to administer the country. Chaos was the predictable result. For at least six weeks after the invasion, looters had access to every significant public institution, except for the

---

* Ansar al-Islam, a group affiliated with al-Qaeda, did have a base in the mountainous no man's land between Iran and the parts of Iraq controlled by the pro-American Kurdistan Regional Government.

Oil Ministry, which U.S. troops did guard. At the same time, the Bush administration fumbled from a plan to set up an interim Iraqi government (announced May 5) to a plan for a multi-year occupation (announced to the Iraqi leaders May 16). The confusion is directly attributable to a president who boasted he was the decider and yet never knew these were the sort of critical questions a president is supposed to decide. Chaos created an opening for Saddam's Baathist cadres to regroup and for al-Qaeda and its allies to enter Iraq. Al-Qaeda and other Sunni fundamentalists discovered they could kill both Americans and Shiites in Iraq. The fighting derailed Defense Secretary Donald Rumsfeld's plans for a rapid drawdown of U.S. troops. The continued presence of large numbers of American troops drew new recruits to al-Qaeda and made it a symbol of Sunni resistance to the infidel in Iraq and elsewhere in the Sunni world. While American troops had armored vehicles and secure bases, ordinary Iraqi Shiites did not. Al-Qaeda specialized in mass bombings that killed large numbers of adherents to a branch of Islam they see as heretical. Eventually these attacks triggered a civil war. Iraq did become the central front in the war on terror with the additional complication that the terrorists appeared to be winning.

When he ordered U.S. forces into Iraq in 2003, President Bush proclaimed the freedom of the Iraqi people to be his goal. The administration even gave the military campaign the code name "Operation Iraqi Freedom." Almost immediately after ousting Saddam Hussein, the Bush administration began a major effort to remake Iraq into a free society. L. Paul (Jerry) Bremer III, the Bush appointee as head of the Coalition Provisional Authority (CPA) for Iraq, moved quickly to abolish the old regime's repressive apparatus: the Iraqi Army, the security services, and the Baath party. He went on to impose a sweeping lifetime ban on senior Baathists in the public service, to write an interim constitution replete with guarantees of personal freedom, and to remake Iraq in line with an American conservative's vision of a market-oriented free society. Five years later, President Bush's speeches about Iraq were still laced with references to freedom and a free Iraq.

Democracy does not exist in Arab Iraq. Shiite religious parties rule Iraq's south, where they have created their own theocratic dictatorships. The good ones resemble Iran; others are a Shiite version of Taliban rule in Afghanistan where women do not work, girls do not go to school, and any deviance in dress or conduct means death. In 2008, al-Qaeda lost control of many Sunni areas. The new rulers were the same Baathists who had ruled in 2003, and were no more democratic than they had ever been.

By 2008, the United States was not fighting for democracy or freedom in Iraq. President Bush was sending U.S. troops into battle in southern Iraq to help Shiite theocrats fight their Shiite rivals and in central Iraq to serve alongside Baathist militiamen.

The Iraq War was intended to transform Iraq from brutal dictatorship into the Arab world's first real democracy. President Bush fully expected a democratic Iraq would be both a role model for other Middle Eastern countries and a subversive force against the region's authoritarian rulers. Envisioning a replay of the 1989 Eastern European revolutions, where elections in Poland set in motion a process that swept away the Berlin Wall and the Soviet Union, the Iraq War's neoconservative architects imagined the quick collapse of Syria's Baathist regime, the growing strength of prodemocracy forces in Iran, and ultimately the replacement of pro-American autocrats in Saudi Arabia and Egypt with pro-American democrats.

Iraq, however, did not become a democracy. Instead it split apart and descended into a brutal civil war. While the Bush administration boasts of the freedoms incorporated into Iraq's constitution, prodemocracy reformers see that those freedoms exist only on paper. The constitution is a road map to partition, consolidating Kurdistan's position as a de facto independent state and legalizing its separate government, laws, and army. Furthermore, the constitution leaves the door open for the Shiites and Sunnis to form their own regions with exactly the same powers as Kurdistan, and indeed, the Shiites are moving to do just that.

Far from inspiring other Middle Eastern countries to move toward democracy, these developments in Iraq have strengthened the region's hard-line regimes. In 2005, Syria's Baathist regime, led by Bashar al-Assad, was in deep trouble, having been caught red-handed in the Beirut assassination of former Lebanese prime minister Rafik Hariri. Three years later, the regime appears more entrenched than ever. In 2003, Iran had a liberal, reform-oriented president. However, the Bush administration's combination of harsh rhetoric toward Iran and manifest incompetence in Iraq helped elect hard-liner Mahmoud Ahmadinejad as Iran's president. In spite of his bizarre utterances, Ahmadinejad has shrewdly used confrontation with the Bush administration to convert his largely powerless office into a more significant one.

Iran is the winner of the war that George W. Bush lost. Iran's closest allies in the world are the Shiite religious parties that, thanks to the American invasion, today run Iraq's central government. The Badr Organization, a Shiite militia, dominates

the upper ranks of the Iraqi Army and effectively controls the
national police. Iran founded the Badr Organization (then the
Badr Corps) in Iran in the 1980s, providing funding, training,
arms, and officers. Iran's President Ahmadinejad has said his
country will fill the vacuum left by the United States in Iraq,
and he is well placed to do so.

George W. Bush's strategic gift to Iran comprises that country's biggest gains in four centuries. In addition to a leading role
in Iraq's central government, Iran's Shiite allies now control
most of southern Iraq. This puts Iran in the position to dominate the world's largest oil reserves. Iran's influence now extends
across the vast oil fields of southern Iraq to the borders of Kuwait and Saudi Arabia's Eastern Province. The former is itself an
important oil producer while Saudi Arabia's Eastern Province,
home to the kingdom's Shiites, has the country's most important oil fields. Iran is in a position to undermine the Sunni king
of Shiite-majority Bahrain, the site of the major U.S. naval base
in the Persian Gulf, and has become an important—and not
helpful—player in the Levant thanks to its support for the Lebanese Shiite party Hezbollah.

Making the Middle East democratic was also intended
to make it safer for Israel. But just as Iran has emerged as the
unintended beneficiary of the changes wrought by the Iraq
War, Israel is the loser. Instead of a democratic Palestine and a
democratic Lebanon, it confronts two radical movements on
the other side of its borders: Hamas and Hezbollah. By 2003,
Saddam Hussein posed only a hypothetical future threat to Israel. Iraq had neither the rockets that could reach Israel nor the
weapons of mass destruction (WMD) that could do it harm. A
much-empowered Iran provided Hezbollah with the hundreds
of rockets that actually struck Israel in 2006. Saddam provided

cash payments to the families of Palestinian suicide bombers, but Iran's president publicly doubts that the Holocaust ever took place and threatens the existence of Israel. And, unlike Iraq, Iran has an active WMD program that will give it the possibility of making nuclear weapons.

The Iraq War fit into a neoconservative security doctrine based on preserving American preeminence in world affairs. Having the United States come out of the Cold War as the world's sole superpower, the ideologues shaping the Bush security policy were determined to prevent any "peer competitor" from emerging. A swift victory in Iraq was one way of confirming the unrivaled power of the United States.

The neoconservatives, however, failed to consider that military strength is only one aspect of power, and not necessarily the most important. (Russia is not a superpower even though it has all of the Soviet Union's nukes.) American power comes not only from the strength of our military and the size of our economy, but also from the respect people around the world have for America and its leaders. Because of George W. Bush, the United States lost respect everywhere in the world, with the possible exceptions of Albania and Iraqi Kurdistan. In few places was the decline as dramatic as in Turkey.

In 2000, the United States enjoyed a 60 percent approval rating among Turks. This favorable rating was due to many things: the historic alliance with Turkey going back to the early years of the Cold War, Turkey's self-identification with the West and Western values, and general admiration for America's charismatic president, Bill Clinton. By 2007, just 9 percent of Turks approved of the United States and a whopping 83 percent disapproved. The American invasion of Iraq, the Bush administration's arrogant dismissal of Turkish concerns about the war, the

obvious American incompetence on display in Iraq, and disdain
for George W. Bush have all contributed to this seismic shift in
Turkish public opinion. While some of Bush's defenders have
tried to argue that world opinion does not matter as long as
America does the right thing (by their lights), this is untrue.
In October 2007, the Turkish parliament ignored American
objections and authorized Turkish troops to cross the border
into Iraq in pursuit of the PKK, a Turkish Kurdish rebel group.
While Turkey had legitimate concerns about PKK activities,
the Bush administration rightly worried that a Turkish invasion
of northern Iraq could bring chaos to Iraqi Kurdistan, the one
stable and pro-Western part of the country. With 160,000 U.S.
troops stretched thin by the fighting elsewhere in Iraq, Turkey's
threatened invasion was not the act of a friend. That Turkey
could contemplate such a course of action was one concrete example of the price America pays for its lost esteem.

The Iraq War was intended to project American strength in
the world. Instead it revealed weakness. Foreigners who thought
the CIA was omniscient and omnipotent learned that it could
not distinguish trailers for weather balloons from mobile biological weapons laboratories and that the word of a drunken
defector code named "Curveball" was considered dispositive.
The U.S. president and secretary of state presented as the absolute truth conclusions drawn from fragmentary intelligence
and crudely forged documents and, as a result, both foreigners and Americans now doubt administration warnings on Iran.
The U.S. administration of postwar Iraq was so inept that it
undermined the very notion of American efficiency and administrative competence. Even the ability of the U.S. military to
strike fear in potential adversaries (a reputation that was central

to America's successes in the Balkans in the 1990s) was undermined by its inability to contain an insurgency that had only shallow support in Iraq itself.

Karl Rove, Bush's political strategist, conceived of the Iraq War as part of broader political strategy that plays on the Republicans' presumed political advantage on national security and fighting terrorism. This was intended to keep the Republicans in power for a generation. Instead, the Republicans lost control of the House and Senate in the 2006 midterm elections (losing an astounding twenty-four of the thirty-three Senate seats that were up for grabs) and appear poised to lose the White House in 2008.

George W. Bush has refused to take responsibility for the fiasco he has created. He has repeatedly said he will leave the problem of Iraq to his successor. In effect, he plans to run out the clock on Iraq. Americans should be outraged that the men and women of the U.S. military are being asked to risk their lives in pursuit of goals in Iraq that Bush no longer pursues but will not admit he has abandoned.

Aside from saying he used inappropriate language (it was a mistake, he now says, to have taunted Iraq's insurgents in 2003 with the phrase "Bring them on"), President Bush acknowledges no specific mistakes in Iraq. His neoconservative allies are laying the groundwork to blame the next president—presumably a Democrat—for losing Iraq. Neoconservative think tanks, such as the American Enterprise Institute, and publications, such as the *Weekly Standard,* now produce a steady flow of reports, articles, and op-eds explaining how the United States has turned the corner in Iraq and is now winning. When the next president withdraws, those who actually lost the war will be making the case that defeat was snatched from the jaws of victory. While it is preposterous that there should be any debate as to who lost Iraq, the next president would ignore the matter at his peril.

The next president will, of course, face greater challenges than countering partisan assaults. He will have to decide exactly how to withdraw from Iraq and how to deal with what is left behind. The next president will need an Iran strategy that aims at avoiding having to choose between a nuclear-armed Iran and war with Iran. He will need to refocus attention on the war on terror and on nuclear proliferation. President Bush has chosen to ignore the inconvenient truth that Pakistan, an American ally, is both the world's most promiscuous proliferator of nuclear technology and a breeding ground for Sunni fundamentalist terrorists, including al-Qaeda. Pakistan is more than episodically chaotic; it is at risk of becoming a failed state and the next president will need to apply both strategy and attention to events in the world's second most populous Islamic state.

The next president's most difficult challenge will be restoring American prestige and leadership in the world. U.S. approval ratings will go up the moment George Bush leaves office, but, no matter how appealing and effective the next president may be, he is unlikely to restore America's standing in the world to what is was in 2000. The next president must focus on the larger implications of the issues thrown into stark relief by the American failure in Iraq: other countries have internal divisions comparable to those that led to the breakup of Iraq. It is time to rethink our reflexive commitment to the continuation of every country now on the planet and to reconsider our bias against self-determination. We need to figure out how to do postconflict nation building in a competent manner, because as much as our leaders insist this is not America's mission, it is certain to be. Finally, the new president must look at the institutions of our own government that failed so miserably in the Iraq crisis: an intelligence system that got us into a war it didn't tell us we would likely lose; a hopelessly politicized Pentagon where the most senior uniformed officers lacked the courage to give their bosses unpopular military advice; a diplomatic service starved for resources and ignored even when right; and a White House headed by a president who claimed it was his job to decide and then not only did not make the most fateful decisions of his administration but never realized these were matters for a president to decide. Above all, the next president will need a national security strategy based on a realistic appraisal of the world and a set of objectives prioritized according to importance, risk, and available resources.

In short, we need to be smart. A superpower that makes national security decisions based on ideological convictions and wishful thinking will not long be a superpower.

The Iraq War was intended to change the Middle East and so it did. The Middle East therefore must be the initial focus of the U.S. effort to repair the damage done by the Iraq War.

1

The Potemkin Surge

At the beginning of 2007, President Bush announced a new strategy for Iraq. The United States would increase or "surge" its troops there by an additional 20,000. The new troops, the president announced in January, would be deployed to Baghdad and to Anbar Governorate, the purely Sunni province that was the seat of the insurgency. U.S. troops would no longer live in sprawling bases making patrols into the dangerous terrain beyond the barbed wire; instead they would live with their Iraqi counterparts at police stations and other locales, providing training and mentoring. To implement his new strategy, Bush appointed General David Petraeus to be the top U.S. commander in Iraq. Petraeus, a West Point graduate and Princeton Ph.D., had served two previous tours in Iraq and had written a manual on counterinsurgency. Two months before announcing the surge, President Bush had fired Defense Secretary Donald Rumsfeld and appointed in his place an experienced government official, former CIA director Robert Gates. With a more professional team and a new strategy, Bush hoped that violence would decline sufficiently so as to give Iraqis the time and space to make progress on the political and military fronts.

The surge was, as it turned out, fortuitously timed. The Sunni insurgency had begun in April 2003 in Anbar after two incidents in which U.S. forces killed Iraqi civilians. (The air force killed twenty-two in the bombing of a Ramadi home after receiving false intelligence that Saddam was hiding there, and in the other incident Marines in Fallujah fired into a crowd after being shot at, killing at least thirteen.) Initially, the resistance was a combination of angry tribal leaders, other Baathists, and the Saddam fedayeen, a Baathist paramilitary. Over the ensuing months, Salafi jihadis,* including those associated with al-Qaeda, joined the fight. Some were foreigners and many more were Iraqi Sunnis.

As-Shoura is the holiest day for Shiite Muslims, marking as it does the anniversary of the massacre of Imam Hussein, the Prophet's grandson, near Karbala in 680. March 2, 2004, was the first time in twenty-nine years that Iraq's Shiite majority was free to commemorate the holiday with the traditional pilgrimages to Karbala and other Shiite shrines. That day, al-Qaeda suicide bombers blew themselves up among the pilgrims in Karbala and at the Khadimiya shrine in Baghdad, killing at least 180. Subsequent attacks on Shiite civilians killed thousands and, in 2006, al-Qaeda blew up the golden-domed Askariya shrine in

---

* Salafi jihadis practice a puritanical and austere form of Sunni Islam. They consider it a religious duty to wage war against infidels and apostates, including Shiites and Muslims who deviate from strict adherence to their version of orthodoxy.

Samarra, provoking Shiite attacks on Sunnis and escalating a Sunni-Shiite civil war already under way.

By attacking the Shiites, whom they see as belonging to a heretical branch of Islam, al-Qaeda in Mesopotamia (as the Iraqi affiliate began to style itself) transformed the insurgency from being primarily an anti-American campaign into a Sunni-Shiite religious war. Initially, the attacks on the Shiites served the purposes of the Baathists and the Anbar tribal leaders. It sowed chaos in the new Iraq and targeted a group the Baathists saw as Iranian pawns. Many experts believe the Baathists were behind some of the attacks on the Shiites and used al-Qaeda as a cover for their own actions.

Thanks to the spectacular and brutal nature of its attacks and to its public relations skills, al-Qaeda in Mesopotamia (AQM) became the most visible part of the insurgency. As it and the other Salafi jihadis became stronger, they challenged the traditional power structure in Anbar and other Sunni areas. AQM assassinated local chieftains and, in some instances, forced their daughters to marry AQM fighters. (Such marriages were thinly disguised rapes.) By 2006, many of Anbar's leaders were fed up with al-Qaeda and they turned to the Americans for help. Even though these Sunni leaders had been insurgents or insurgent sympathizers, General Petraeus responded favorably. Beginning in Anbar, the Sunni tribesmen formed militias that they called the Sunni Awakening, or, later, the Sons of Iraq. The United States agreed to pay the salaries of the militiamen, as well as generous subsidies to the tribal leaders. In a matter of months, they suppressed, but did not eliminate, al-Qaeda in Anbar. And because al-Qaeda was now fighting fellow Sunnis, it no longer had the resources—or safe bases—to plot deadly attacks on the Shiites. By September 2007, there had been a real change in Iraq. Sectarian killing was down and Baghdad's morgue actually had space to spare.

President Bush decided to make a victory lap—not to Baghdad but to Anbar, which had been the epicenter of the Sunni insurgency. En route to a summit meeting in Australia, Air Force One touched down at the governorate's remote al-Asad air base. A year before, a presidential visit to Anbar—even to a heavily guarded and remote air base—would have been unthinkably dangerous. Back in 2006, the Marines had described Anbar in a leaked intelligence report as lost to al-Qaeda and now the U.S. president was there. Frederick Kagan, the American Enterprise Institute scholar who was the intellectual architect of the surge strategy, saw the visit as vindication of his approach. The Bush visit, he enthused, "should be recognized as at least the Gettysburg of this war."

In his weekly radio address just after the trip, Bush attributed the success both to U.S. troops and to the people of Anbar.

> Local citizens soon saw what life under al-Qaeda meant for them. The terrorists brutalized the people of Anbar and killed those who opposed their dark ideology. So the tribal sheiks of Anbar came together to fight al-Qaeda. They asked for support from the coalition and the Iraqi government, and we responded. Together we have driven al-Qaeda out of strongholds in Anbar. The level of violence is down. Local governments are meeting again. Young Sunnis are joining the police and army. And normal life is returning. The people of Anbar have seen that standing up to the terrorists and extremists leads to a better life. And Anbar has shown

that improving security is the first step toward achieving economic progress and political reconciliation.

Sheik Abdul-Sattar Abu Risha, the local Sunni leader in Ramadi, was the man most responsible for assembling the Anbar Sunni Awakening and the White House wanted a picture of the president with the local hero. No one told Abu Risha this since the president's visit was, for security reasons, a closely guarded secret. A photograph from their September 3 meeting shows a grinning president, flanked by a smiling General Petraeus and Defense Secretary Gates, shaking hands with Abu Risha. The sheik looks as if he wants to be anyplace else. Ten days later, an al-Qaeda bomb killed Abu Risha near his Ramadi home.

In addition to claiming victory prematurely (not for the first time), Bush misrepresented other key facts in his radio address. The Sunni Awakening in Anbar did not seek support from the Iraq government, which it despises as much as it does al-Qaeda. The Iraqi government was not letting significant numbers of young Sunnis into the Iraqi Army and police precisely because this would put its security in the hands of the enemy.

General Petraeus has emphasized that the United States is not arming the Awakening, but is simply paying salaries. The official explanation is that all members have personal weapons as allowed under Iraqi law but the real reason is that the Iraqi government opposes arming the Awakening. The Awakening's "personal weapons" are far more lethal than what might commonly be understood by the phrase. As former insurgents, the Awakening militiamen have an array of weapons, many of which came, ironically and indirectly, from General Petraeus. In 2004, Petraeus, as the American general responsible for building a new Iraqi Army, oversaw the distribution of assault rifles and other weapons. Inexplicably, the United States failed to record the serial numbers, and Sunni recruits turned many of these over to the insurgents. In 2007, many of those same insurgents were using those weapons to fight alongside the United States against al-Qaeda.

In the second half of 2007, the Awakening spread to Baghdad and, with U.S. support, took back the city's Sunni neighborhoods from al-Qaeda and the other Salafi jihadis. Shops, playgrounds, and restaurants reopened and parents once again dared to send their children to school. In Baghdad, the Awakening also provided Sunnis with some defense against Shiite death squads and criminal gangs, which had, along with al-Qaeda, made life intolerable for most Sunnis in the capital.

Still, in Baghdad and in Anbar, the gains were much less than claimed by the administration's boosters. Al-Qaeda continued to assassinate Awakening militiamen and leaders, stage suicide bomb attacks on Shiites, launch mortar attacks into Baghdad's heavily fortified international zone (the Green Zone), and place improvised explosive devices (IEDs) that kill Americans. Eighteen months into Bush's new strategy, Baghdad was still far too dangerous for an American—or an Iraqi politician—to travel around except with heavily armed escorts. Pushed out of Baghdad and Anbar, al-Qaeda had, at the start of 2008, stepped up operations in Mosul, Iraq's third-largest city, a tense place divided by the Tigris river between a Sunni west bank and a Kurdish east bank. Fighting al-Qaeda resembles the "whack-a-mole" game. Knocked down in one place, al-Qaeda pops up in another.

The decline in violence that followed the surge raises two questions: If the surge troops really made the difference, what will happen after the troops go? And, if the decline in violence is due to other factors, such as the Awakening, how durable are the gains?

When George W. Bush toppled Saddam Hussein's regime on April 9, 2003, he ended eighty years of Sunni rule. Because he had made no plans for how to govern Iraq or provide public security, he left a void. In the Sunni areas, tribal leaders, Baathists, and religious extremists exploited the absence of authority to create the insurgency. In the Shiite areas, clerics and religious parties rushed to fill the void.

Days after Saddam's regime collapsed in southern Iraq, Iranian-based Shiite religious parties, and their militias, moved back to Iraq. The most prominent of these were the Supreme Council for the Islamic Revolution in Iraq (SCIRI) and Dawa, a revolutionary Shiite party founded in the 1950s. Both had close ties to Iran. SCIRI was founded by the Ayatollah Ruhollah Khomeini in Tehran in 1982. The Iranians also created SCIRI's militia, the Badr Corps (renamed after liberation as the Badr Organization on the pretense that its mission had changed to social work). Iran funded, trained, armed, and officered the Badr Corps and still has the closest possible ties to it. Working with local clerics, SCIRI and Dawa set up local administrations that restarted essential services and in which the Badr Corps provided security. They also began the process of transforming the south into a theocratic state.

Although closely associated with Iran and theocratic, SCIRI and Dawa represented the Shiite establishment. Jerry Bremer, head of the Coalition Provisional Authority, recognized them as such. He appointed SCIRI and Dawa leaders to his Iraqi Governing Council and placed their nominees in key positions in the interim Iraqi government and the reconstituted bureaucracy.

He also helped them infiltrate their cadres into the Iraqi Army and police. In 2005, SCIRI and Dawa formed an electoral alliance with other Shiite parties that won an absolute majority in Iraq's Transitional National Assembly.

As SCIRI and Dawa were taking over the south in April 2003, Moqtada al-Sadr, a pudgy thirty-year-old cleric, was beginning a movement that was to challenge their preeminence as well as the American occupation. While his own religious credentials were scant, Moqtada came from a line of revered Shiite ayatollahs. The family had the mantle of martyrdom since Saddam had murdered Moqtada's father, brothers, and grandfather. Moqtada found support in the south but his base was in the Shiite parts of Baghdad, and in particular Sadr City, the sprawling Shiite slum of two million that had been renamed for his father the day Saddam fell (it had been Saddam City). Sadr's fiery sermons and the memory of his martyred family won him thousands of adherents, particularly among Sadr City's slum dwellers. With the Americans preoccupied with the growing Sunni insurgency, he established in 2003 his own militia, the Mahdi Army (named after the last Shiite Imam, who disappeared in 878 and whose return Shiites believe will herald the end of the world). In 2004, the Mahdi Army fought the Americans in Najaf, winning far more recruits through its heroic stand than it lost in battle. By the end of 2006, the Mahdi Army was by far Iraq's largest militia with more men claiming to be part of it than in the Iraqi Army. It controlled most of Shiite Baghdad (70 percent of the city) and parts of the south, including neighborhoods in Basra. In some places, including Basra, it imposed Taliban-type rule. In Baghdad, the Mahdi Army was actively engaged in a campaign to drive Sunnis from the city, using death squads and other terror tactics to accomplish the mission.

The Bush administration intended the surge not only to fight the Sunni insurgency but also to break the Mahdi Army's control over Baghdad. It was a risky strategy since the United States was, in effect, doubling its enemies in Iraq with only 15 percent more troops. However, instead of resisting the Americans, Moqtada al-Sadr ordered the Mahdi Army to stand down at the start of the surge, and for the most part it did. Al-Sadr made the obvious calculation that there was no point in fighting the Americans since they would be, sooner or later, gone. By standing down his forces, he conserved them for future battles against Shiite rivals and the Sunnis. (Some Mahdi Army commanders did not follow Moqtada's orders and ended up fighting U.S. troops. From Moqtada's point of view this was not a bad outcome. The Mahdi Army grew so rapidly that Moqtada no longer controlled parts of it. The Americans, in effect, helped purge the renegades.)

Even after standing down, the Mahdi Army is a potent force in Sadr City and other Shiite neighborhoods in Baghdad. There is every reason to suppose that, once the U.S. troops leave, the Mahdi Army will retake neighborhoods and resume its campaign of terror aimed at driving Sunnis from Baghdad. If so, the surge will have bought a respite in Baghdad's violence but not the end.

Even if Iraqi Army units and police replace the Mahdi Army in Baghdad, it will not mean the end to sectarian fighting in the city. The Iraqi police and, to a lesser extent, the army are also sectarian institutions. Their loyalty is mostly to the establishment Shiite religious parties. These parties also have death squads and, while they are more subtle about it, they would also like to see Baghdad become a Shiite city.

In contrast to what happened on the Shiite side of the line, the surge's gains against al-Qaeda may be more durable. The Bush administration wants the Awakening incorporated into the Iraqi Army and police. This is consistent with the American vision of a single Iraqi people and of a nonsectarian Iraqi security force. For the most part, the Sunni militiamen want to be included in the Iraqi security forces since this means a higher and more regular salary. The Sunnis think of themselves as real Iraqis (which, in their view, the Shiites are not) and the true defenders of the country. Moreover, the Awakening leaders know that even when wearing the uniforms of an Iraqi soldier or policeman, their militiamen will still be loyal to their Sunni leaders, and not the Shiite chain of command.

Iraqi Shiites see the Awakening much as the Awakening sees itself: as the instrument of Iraq's Sunnis and a threat to Shiite majority rule. In spite of a promise made to the United States to include the Awakening in Iraq's security forces, the Iraqi government has not done so. In late 2007, Brigadier General Jim Huggins, who oversaw the Iraqi police in the Sunni belt south of Baghdad, submitted three thousand names of mostly Sunni recruits, but including a few hundred Shiites, to the Iraqi government for approval. The four hundred approved were all Shiites. By the end of 2007, only a few thousand of the estimated sixty-five thousand Awakening militiamen had, in fact, been incorporated into the Iraqi Army or police. The Shiites understand that an army or police uniform and a regular salary will not make the Sunnis loyal to a Shiite-led Iraq. In December 2007, Iraq's national government stressed it did not want the Awakening to become a permanent institution. For this reason, it said it would not provide the Awakening with headquarters and would disband it as soon as possible. Said Defense Minister Abdul Qadir al-Obaidi, "We completely reject the Awakening becoming a third military organization."*

Up to one-half of the Awakening militiamen were part of the insurgency, battling the Iraqi government and its American allies. Joining forces with the Americans provided these Sunnis with clear tactical advantages: regular salaries, the departure of the Shiite army from their areas, and U.S. support for crushing al-Qaeda rivals. But this is a conversion of convenience. The Awakening's view of the Iraqi government is no less hostile than when its members were planting roadside bombs, ambushing government forces, and executing kidnapped Iraqi Army recruits and police. As General Huggins told *USA Today*, "If these [Awakening members] aren't pulled into the security forces, then we have to wonder if we're just arming the next Sunni resistance."

At their core, the Awakening are Sunni Arab nationalists—and in many cases unreconstructed Baathists—who see Iraq's government as the agent of their great national enemy, Iran. Iraq's Sunnis and Shiites know full well that Iraq's civil war has not miraculously ended, and both are preparing for the next round.

There was another reason for the decline in violence in Baghdad in 2007 that had nothing to do with the surge, the Awakening, or the Mahdi Army stand-down. From 2003 on, Sunnis and Shiites targeted each other in mixed neighborhoods so that those neighborhoods became purely Sunni or purely Shiite. By

---

* The other two military organizations are the Iraqi army and Kurdistan peshmerga.

mid-2007, there were almost no mixed neighborhoods left in Iraq. Violence declined because Shiite and Sunni gunmen had fewer people left to terrorize and kill. And, while the decline in violence in Iraq in 2007 was real, it hardly equaled peace. By the end of 2007, killings from death squads and suicide bombings had simply returned to the levels of March 2006, now considered the first month of full-scale civil war in Iraq.

The surge had two objectives beyond reducing the violence. First, it was intended to provide a breathing space so as to allow Iraq's government to enact a program of national reconciliation that would accommodate enough Sunnis so as to isolate the insurgents. Second, it was intended to provide time for training Iraqi forces—including by working and living with U.S. troops—so that the Iraqis could take over security when the surge ended and U.S. forces drew down.

Iraq's national reconciliation program involves legislation and political actions to make Iraq's Sunnis feel they have a place in new Shiite Iraq. These include an oil revenue–sharing law (to guarantee the Sunnis a share of Iraq's oil revenues, which comes from production in the Shiite south or Kurdistan); holding provincial elections (the Sunnis boycotted the January 2005 provincial and parliamentary elections, which left them underrepresented even in Sunni-majority provinces); revising Iraq's constitution (the Sunnis want a more centralized state); revising the ban on public sector employment of former Baathists (Sunnis dominated the upper ranks of the Baath party and of the Saddam-era public service); and a fair distribution of reconstruction funds. The U.S. Congress has, by law, linked U.S. strategy on Iraq and financial support of the Iraqi government to progress on these benchmarks and other steps. Iraq's Council of Representatives passed the first benchmark, a law on de-Baathification, only in January 2008. That law was passed by the Shiite block over the vociferous opposition of the Sunnis it was supposed to reconcile. The Sunnis opposed the de-Baathification law because it made their situation worse.

When Iraq's leaders failed to implement the benchmarks, U.S. politicians and editorial page writers criticized them as quarrelsome, lazy, and lacking vision. If only Iraq had a Mandela, goes a common refrain.* But the problem in Iraq is not the absence of a Mandela. Rather, it is the depth of the divisions that exist in the country.

Rehiring former Baathists is a case in point. For Americans, this seems exceptionally straightforward. According to the conventional wisdom, CPA administrator Bremer made a huge mistake when he banned from public service people who had served at the top four ranks in the Baath party. While intending to weed out the truly evil, he inadvertently fired people who joined only for careerist reasons, including doctors, teachers, and the like. Disaffected, these Baathists turned to the insurgency, but if the ban were removed, they might be reconciled.

If only it were so simple. Abdul Aziz al-Hakim leads the Supreme Islamic Iraqi Council (SIIC, which was SCIRI until being renamed in 2007). It is Iraq's leading Shiite party and a critical component of Prime Minister al-Maliki's coalition. He is the sole survivor of eight brothers. During Saddam's rule, Baathists executed six of them. On August 29, 2003, a suicide bomber, possibly linked to the Baathists, blew up his last surviving brother (and who was his predecessor as SCIRI leader),

---

* Apologists for Iraq's current leaders rightly note that Saddam killed all of Iraq's would-be Mandelas.

at the shrine of Ali in Najaf. Moqtada al-Sadr, Hakim's main rival, comes from Iraq's other prominent Shiite religious family. Saddam's Baath regime murdered his father and two brothers in 1999. Earlier, in April 1980, the regime had arrested Moqtada's father-in-law and the father-in-law's sister—the Grand Ayatollah Baqir al-Sadr and Bint al-Huda. Shiites believe the ayatollah was forced to watch as Baath security men raped and killed his sister. They then set fire to the ayatollah's beard before driving nails into his head. De-Baathification is an intensely personal issue for Iraq's two most powerful Shiite political leaders, as it is for hundreds of thousands of their followers who suffered similar atrocities.

Iraq's Shiite-crafted de-Baathification law did not give back Sunnis their old jobs, which had, in any event, been filled by Shiites. The law does force the retirement of former Baathists still working in security-related ministries. It restores the pensions that Bremer recklessly took away but does nothing to include Sunnis in the new Iraq. These inconvenient facts did not stop George Bush from citing the law as "an encouraging sign" of progress in his 2008 State of the Union address.

Iraq's Shiite leaders opposed provincial elections because they knew what such elections would likely bring. The Sunnis boycotted the January 2005 elections, which were for both the Transitional National Assembly and for the governorate councils. This left Sunnis unrepresented in mixed-population governorates such as Baghdad and Diyala, northeast of Baghdad. Because of the boycott, Kurdish parties run Nineveh, which includes Mosul and is the largest Sunni-majority governorate.

The Bush administration has pushed for provincial elections, which neither the Kurds nor the establishment Shiites want, in order to make the Sunnis feel more included in the new

Iraq. But in its effort to accommodate the Sunnis, the Bush administration seemed never to have contemplated the impact of elections on the Shiites. Moqtada al-Sadr did not run candidates in the January 2005 elections, thus allowing SCIRI (now SIIC) to end up controlling Baghdad and seven of the nine southern governorates. Iraq's decentralized constitution gives the governorates enormous powers and significant shares of the national budget, if they choose to exercise these powers. It was hard to discern the rationale for an administration strategy that would hand Baghdad, and possibly some southern governorates, over to the most radically anti-American Shiite leader in Iraq. In addition, Moqtada al-Sadr's electoral success would seem unlikely to make Sunnis feel more warmly toward the new Iraq.

Under U.S. pressure, Iraq's Council of Representatives passed the provincial elections law in February 2008. Far from being a step toward national reconciliation, the law's consideration in the Iraqi parliament underscored the lack of trust among Iraq's three communities. At the same time as the provincial election law was being considered, Iraq's Council of Representatives was also considering the budget and an amnesty law. Arab Parliamentarians wanted to cut Kurdistan's share of the budget from a previously agreed 17 percent, while Shiite members were reluctant to pass an amnesty law that would have freed many Sunnis. The Kurds were afraid that if the provincial elections and amnesty laws went before the budget, the Sunnis and enough Shiites would vote against the Kurdish earmark to defeat it. The Sunnis were afraid that, if the budget went first, the Shiites might double-cross them on the amnesty law or the provincial elections law. Since no group trusted the others to keep a bargain, it was agreed to vote on all three laws as a single package. As it happened, the Shiites did double-cross the Sunnis. After the laws passed the Council of Representatives, they were sent to Iraq's three-man presidency council* individually for signature. Shiite vice president Adel Abdul Mahdi of SIIC vetoed the provincial elections law. It required the personal intervention of Vice President Dick Cheney, who visited Iraq on March 19 for the five-year anniversary of the start of the Iraq War, to persuade Abdul Mahdi to sign the bill. The elections were scheduled for October 1, 2008, but are likely to be postponed. It remains a fair bet that they will not be held.

The most significant benchmarks concern matters that divide Kurds and Arabs. Implementing these benchmarks does nothing to address issues between Sunnis and Shiites that are at the root of the Iraq conflict. They are certain, however, to increase tensions between Arabs and Kurds, two communities that are currently at peace with each other. It is a measure of how disconnected the Bush administration is from reality that it pursues policies likely to create new conflicts in the name of national reconciliation. Ironically, the Bush administration is doing almost nothing about the territorial dispute between Kurdistan and Arab Iraq, which is the one issue that does need to be resolved between the two communities.

Revenue sharing and constitutional revision are the two benchmarks that most clearly separate the Kurds from the Arabs. The first can be finessed but the second cannot. Both expose the irreconcilable differences that exist in Iraq.

Iraq's constitution provides that revenues from existing oil fields should be divided among regions and governorates

---

* Iraq's constitution establishes a presidency council consisting of the President and two Vice Presidents. Currently, the president is a Kurd and the two vice presidents are a Sunni and a Shiite. Any of the three can veto a bill.

according to population. The Kurdistan Regional Government interprets this to mean it should get automatically a fixed percentage—currently 17 percent—of all revenues from oil sales. They propose setting up a special Kurdistan account at the New York Federal Reserve bank into which their share of Iraqi oil revenues is deposited. The Arabs say Kurdistan's allotment should be included in the Iraqi budget and voted by the parliament. They also want the Baghdad Ministry of Finance to oversee how Kurdistan spends its money and for Baghdad ministries to supervise the activities of their Kurdistan counterparts. The Kurds see this as an Arab effort to claw back their constitutional rights and to diminish their autonomy. Because of high oil prices, Iraq is receiving much more revenue than it is actually spending in the federal budget. The Kurds want 17 percent of those revenues, while the Arab Iraqis propose to provide only a share of the budget expenditures, a significantly lower amount.

While Arabs and Kurds cannot agree on the principles of revenue sharing, they have agreed to share revenues. Kurdistan gets 17 percent of the budget—less deductions for common expenses such as foreign affairs and reparations payments from the 1991 Gulf War—but the central government has no oversight of Kurdistan expenditures. President Bush has excused the failure to pass the revenue-sharing law by pointing out that sharing is actually happening, but that misses the point. The dispute arises because Kurds and Arabs cannot agree whether Iraq is one country or two entities, Kurdistan and Arab Iraq, co-existing within a single set of lines on a map.

By design, Iraq's constitution creates a federal state with powerful regions and a nearly powerless central government. The constitution has 144 articles, but three matter much more than any others. Article 110 lists the exclusive powers of the federal government: foreign policy, defense policy, international commerce, the federal budget, international waters (mainly the Tigris and the Euphrates), and the regulation of weights and measures. Article 115 makes the laws of Iraq's regions superior to federal law on any matter not mentioned in Article 110. Article 121 reinforces regional primacy by giving regions the right to have their own armies, to have diplomatic representation abroad and, most importantly, to amend or cancel the application of federal law within the region. Thus, regions exercise full power on all matters except those listed as exclusive to the federal government in Article 110, and this is a very short list. Among the powers the federal government does *not* have are taxation, control of natural resources, protection of human rights, and the actual conduct of national security (only national security *policy* is a federal responsibility).

Because they boycotted the 2005 elections for the Transitional National Assembly (the body designated with writing Iraq's constitution), the Sunnis had no influence on these key provisions, which were worked out between Kurdistan President Massoud Barzani and SCIRI leader Abdul Aziz al-Hakim in August 2005.* Had the Sunnis been part of the negotiations, Iraq would not have a constitution as the Kurds, who held a veto on ratification,† would not have accepted a document that

---

* A few days before, Hakim proposed the creation of a single Shiite region covering all nine southern governorates and with the same powers as Kurdistan.

† Under Iraq's American-written interim constitution, Iraq's permanent constitution could only be ratified if approved by a majority of voters and was not rejected by two-thirds of the voters in each of three governorates.

did not codify their de facto independence. In August 2005, the Bush administration understood this and, eager to meet an August 15 deadline for the Transitional Assembly to approve a draft, helped broker the Barzani-Hakim deal.

Two months later, however, the U.S. Ambassador to Iraq, Zalmay Khalilzad, negotiated a new bargain in which the Shiites and Kurds agreed to consider constitutional amendments in exchange for Sunnis agreeing to vote for the constitution's ratification in the upcoming referendum. There was, of course, no agreement on the substance of any amendments as neither the Kurds nor the Shiites were willing to give up on provisions important to their communities. And, the Sunnis did not keep their part of the bargain, voting almost unanimously against ratification.

Nonetheless, the Bush administration insists there is a moral obligation to the Sunnis to revise the constitution. All the Sunni-proposed amendments come at the expense of the Kurds. The Sunnis would expand the exclusive powers of the federal government (and thereby diminish Kurdistan's powers), take away Kurdistan's right to amend federal law as applied in Kurdistan, and declare Iraq to be an Arab state, a move the non-Arab Kurds consider racist and exclusionary. Since Kurdish voters would have to approve these amendments, they obviously will never be adopted.

The Bush administration created a process to amend Iraq's Constitution that was certain to fail. They have made the Kurds

---

There being three Kurdish Governorates, the Kurds could have vetoed a constitution that did not give them what they wanted. The permanent constitution makes it impossible to reduce the powers of a region without the consent of the region.

nervous and left the Sunnis frustrated. And, far from promoting national reconciliation, constitutional revision re-ignites
tensions over differences that are incapable of resolution.*

The press has rightly focused much attention on corruption
and waste in U.S. reconstruction efforts in Iraq. Bush administration political appointees, U.S. military officers, U.S. con-
tractors, Iraqi government officials, and Iraqi security personnel
have all been caught with their hands in the cookie jar. And those
caught represent only the tip of the iceberg for what likely will
turn out to be the biggest theft of taxpayer funds in U.S. history.
But, there is, like everything in Iraq, a sectarian angle to the reconstruction story. In a speech in June 2007 on the Senate floor,
Indiana Republican Richard Lugar reported that Iraq's Shiite-led
government has gone "out of its way to bottle up money budgeted for Sunni provinces" and that the "strident intervention"
of the U.S. Embassy was required in order to get food rations
delivered to Sunni towns. Iraq's Shiite government has been unwilling to spend reconstruction—or even regularly budgeted—
funds in Sunni areas because they believe, not without reason,
that such money supports the Sunni side in the civil war.

For the most part, Iraq's leaders are not personally stubborn
or uncooperative. They find it impossible to reach agreement

---

* Paradoxically, the Bush administration, which originally wanted the central government to have more powers under the permanent constitution,
helped produce a weaker government than necessary. As the constitution
was being drafted in 2005, the United Nations came up with a series of proposals that would have made for more workable sharing of power between
regions and the central government. The U.S. embassy stopped the U.N.
from presenting these proposals because it hoped, unrealistically, for a final
document as centralized as (and textually close to) the 2004 interim constitution written by the Americans.

on the benchmarks because their constituents don't agree on any common vision for Iraq. The Shiites voted twice in 2005 for parties that seek to define Iraq as a Shiite state. By their boycotts and votes the Sunni Arabs have almost unanimously rejected the Shiite vision of Iraq's future, including the new constitution. The Kurds envisage an Iraq that does not include them. In the 2005 parliamentary elections, 99 percent of them voted for Kurdish nationalist parties, and in the January 2005 referendum, 98 percent voted for an independent Kurdistan.

But even if Iraq's politicians could agree to the benchmarks, this wouldn't end the insurgency or the civil war. Sunni insurgents and the Awakening both object to Iraq being run by Shiite religious parties, which they see as installed by the Americans, loyal to Iran, and wanting to define Iraq in a way that excludes the Sunnis. Sunni fundamentalists consider the Shiites apostates who deserve death, not power. The Shiites believe that their democratic majority and their historical suffering under the Baathist dictatorship entitle them to rule. They are not inclined to compromise with Sunnis, whom they see as their long-standing oppressors, especially when they believe most Iraqi Sunnis are sympathetic to the suicide bombers who have killed thousands of ordinary Shiites. The differences are fundamental and cannot be papered over by sharing oil revenues, reemploying ex-Baathists, or revising the constitution. The war is not about those things.

The surge strategy was intended to pave the way for an American exit from Iraq by having U.S. forces train and mentor the Iraqi troops and police, who then would take over security duties from the Americans. If Iraq's army and police are to replace the Americans as providers of security, they need to be neutral guarantors of public order, which in turn assumes that the men in these security forces are somehow immune from the country's sectarian and ethnic divisions. In fact, Iraq's security forces tend to be much more sectarian than the rest of the country.

Iraq's ministry of interior recruited and controls Iraq's national police. The minister in Iraq's first elected government was Bayan Jabr, whose previous job was to head the Badr Corps. Not surprisingly, Jabr recruited Badr Corps militiamen to be the national police. It goes without saying that Sunnis do not trust the national police (nor do rival Shiite militias). In the Shiite parts of Arab Iraq, the local police are tied to the Badr Corps or the Mahdi Army, or in the case of Basra, also to Fadhila, a locally prominent Shiite party associated with a branch of the Sadr movement different from that headed by Moqtada al-Sadr. Both the national police and the local Shiite police have been implicated in the death squads that killed thousands of Sunnis. In 2007, thousands of Sunnis disappeared, typically turning up a few days later as corpses with their eyes gouged out and other signs of torture. American journalists writing about these abductions often noted that, before being killed, the victim had been "forced into a police car by men wearing police uniforms." This was because the abductors quite often were the police.

In the Sunni areas, the local police are tied to the local power structure. Until 2007, many sympathized with the insurgency or were part of it. Some still are insurgents. Others are connected to the tribal leaders and Baathists who created the Awakening. It's not surprising that no Sunni in a Shiite area and no Shiite in a Sunni area would trust the local police to protect his rights or his life.

The Iraqi Army is better than the police but still a very

sectarian institution. Most units are either Sunni or Shiite, with only a handful being mixed. As an institution, the army is the agent of Iraq's sectarian Shiite government and many of the top officers were political activists or militia leaders from the Shiite parties that now rule Iraq. The Sunnis do not trust the national army and, as noted, are developing a rival military with U.S. support.

The Kurds have their own army and police. They do not permit the national army or police on their territory. There are three Kurdish battalions in the Iraqi Army, based in each of Kurdistan's three governorates. In order to win congressional support for the surge, the Bush Administration promised that the Iraqi government would deploy three battalions to Baghdad alongside the surged American presence, and Congress made the arrival of the battalions one of its benchmarks. Since there were no Iraqi units that would reliably follow orders deploying them to Baghdad, the Bush administration sought to send the Iraqi army's Kurdish battalions to the capital. But because the Kurdish battalions do not take orders from the authorities in Baghdad, the Americans needed to get an order from Kurdistan's president, Massoud Barzani. He was extremely reluctant to get the Kurds involved in Iraq's Sunni-Shiite civil war but also wanted to be a loyal U.S. ally. Over the strong opposition of many in the Kurdistan government—and the near unanimous opposition of the Kurdish people and of the troops themselves—Barzani issued the necessary order.

The Kurdistan troops proved a popular success in Baghdad. Both Sunnis and Shiites trusted that the Kurds would not take the side of their sectarian enemy and the Kurds were considerably better trained and more disciplined than their Iraqi Army counterparts. U.S. troops liked serving alongside the Kurdish troops, not least because they knew the Kurds were reliably on the U.S. side and not working secretly with Sunni insurgents or Shiite militiamen. However, no Iraqi in Baghdad saw the Kurds as Iraqis, nor did their U.S. military counterparts. The Bush administration never explained to Congress what was actually going on, and Congress took on face value that the Iraqi government had met the commitment to increase its own troops in Baghdad.

In March 2008, Prime Minister Nouri al-Maliki ordered the Iraqi Army and police to take control of Basra from al-Sadr's forces, who held a substantial part of the city. The operation was poorly planned and over one thousand soldiers and policemen refused to fight. In the end, Iran brokered a cease-fire between the Mahdi Army and the government.

Putting the best possible face on what happened, the Bush administration—which had not been told of the operation in advance—proclaimed it a significant development: even if the operation was not a military success, the Iraqi government was at last going after militias.

But it was not as it appeared. The operation was an effort by SIIC and Dawa to defeat Sadr, a political rival, in advance of the provincial elections that could determine which Shiite faction controls the south. The Iraqi Army, its upper cadres dominated by SIIC, behaved not as a national institution but as the militia of one of the parties. Soldiers refused to fight not out of cowardice but because the Mahdi Army has many supporters among the rank and file in the Iraqi Army. Shiite soldiers live in Iraq's Shiite areas and many fear they might be denounced to the local Sadrists in their own neighborhoods.

Since 2007, violence in Iraq has declined. Less violence, however, is not the same thing as winning.

President Bush has defined the U.S. goal as a democratic, stable, and unified Iraq. Victory is achieving our goals, but by mid-2008, the United States was further from victory than ever.

Iraq had broken apart. Sunnis and Shiites were divided into opposing armed camps. In Iraq's Shiite south and in east Baghdad, Shiite religious parties and their militias exercised effective control. In the Sunni areas, the tribal leaders were, for the most part, the same men who had supported Saddam Hussein. They see Iraq's Shiite leaders as Iranian stooges and enemies of the Iraqi state that had once ruled. The Shiite leaders remember the Sunni leaders as architects of the brutal repression they experienced in Saddam's time.

Kurdistan is not part of Iraq's civil war, but it is also not really part of Iraq. With its own army and flag, airports and airline, Kurdistan functions like the independent state it almost is. Its leaders hold high offices in the Baghdad government but they do all they can to keep Iraq at bay. In January 2005, 98 percent of Iraq's Kurds voted for independence in a nonbinding referendum.

George W. Bush has no plans to unify Iraq because, except rhetorically, unity is not on the administration's agenda. It is, quite simply, too hard to attempt.

Iraq's Shiite religious parties have made southern Iraq into a theocracy. The governorates controlled by SIIC model themselves on Iran; where the Mahdi Army holds sway, the regime more closely resembles Taliban Afghanistan. In central Iraq, America's new best friends are Sunni Baathists. Only Kurdistan is pro-Western, secular, and with some elements of democracy. Bush has largely ignored Kurdistan.

George W. Bush has no plans to promote democracy in Iraq. Doing so would require the United States to dislodge undemocratic allies in Sunni and Shiite territory. Except in his speeches, Bush long ago gave up on a democratic Iraq.

Occasionally, the administration's effort to convince the American people—and perhaps even itself—of progress crosses the line into the absurd. On May 30, 2007, I attended a coalition ceremony in Kurdistan's capital, Erbil, to mark the handover of security in Iraq's three Kurdish provinces from the coalition to the Iraqi government. General Benjamin Mixon, the U.S. commander for northern Iraq, praised the Iraqi government for overseeing all aspects of the handover, drew attention to the "benchmark" now achieved: with the handover, he said, Iraqis now controlled security in seven of Iraq's eighteen provinces.

In fact, nothing was handed over. The only coalition force in Kurdistan is the peshmerga, a disciplined army that fought alongside the Americans in the 2003 campaign to oust Saddam Hussein and is loyal to the Kurdistan government in Erbil. The peshmerga provided security in the three Kurdish provinces before the handover and after. The Iraqi Army has not been on Kurdistan's territory since 1996 and is effectively prohibited from being there. Nor did the Iraqi flag fly at the ceremony. It was banned in Kurdistan.

Although the Erbil handover was a sham that Prince Potemkin might have admired, it was not easily arranged. The Bush administration had wanted the handover to take place before the U.S. congressional elections in November, but it also wanted an Iraqi flag flown at the ceremony and some acknowledgment that Iraq, not Kurdistan, was in charge. The Kurds were prepared to include a reference to Iraq in the ceremony, but they were adamant that there be no Iraqi flags. It took months to work out a compromise ceremony with no flags at all. Thus the ceremony was followed by a military parade without a single flag—an event so unusual that one observer thought it might merit mention in *Ripley's Believe It or Not.*

The Potemkin ceremony in Erbil was simply a more extreme—and comic—version of a campaign mounted throughout 2007 to persuade the American people that the United States is, in fact, winning the Iraq war.

2

Who Lost Iraq?

In spite of the failure to achieve any of America's political objectives in Iraq, President Bush and the war's architects continue to insist the United States is winning in Iraq. Nonetheless, the specter of defeat shapes their thinking in telling ways.

The case for the war is no longer defined by the benefits of winning—a stable Iraq, democracy on the march in the Middle East, the collapse of the evil Iranian and Syrian regimes—but by the consequences of defeat. As President Bush put it, "The consequences of failure in Iraq would be death and destruction in the Middle East and here in America."

Tellingly, the Iraq War's intellectual boosters, while insisting that the battlefield situation turned in America's favor in 2007, have moved to assign blame for defeat. And they have already picked their target: the American people. In the *Weekly Standard*, Tom Donnelly, a fellow at the neoconservative American Enterprise Institute, wrote, "Those who believe the war is already lost—call it the Clinton-Lugar axis—are mounting a surge of their own. Ground won in Iraq becomes ground lost at home." Lugar provoked Donnelly's anger by noting that the American people had lost confidence in Bush's Iraq strategy, as demonstrated by the Democratic takeover of both houses of Congress. This "blame the American people" approach has, through repetition, almost become the accepted explanation for the outcome in Vietnam, attributing defeat to a loss of public support and not to fifteen years of military failure.

Indeed, Vietnam is the image many Americans have of defeat in Iraq. Al-Qaeda would overrun the Green Zone and the last Americans would evacuate from the rooftop of the still-unfinished largest embassy in the world. President Bush feeds on this imagery. In his May 5, 2007, radio address to the nation, he explained:

> If radicals and terrorists emerge from this battle with control of Iraq, they would have control of a nation with massive oil reserves, which they could use to fund their dangerous ambitions and spread their influence. The al-Qaeda terrorists who behead captives or order suicide bombings would not be satisfied to see America defeated and gone from Iraq. They would be emboldened by their victory, protected by their new sanctuary, eager to impose their hateful vision on surrounding countries, and eager to harm Americans.

But there will be no Saigon moment in Iraq. Iraq's Shiite-led government is in no danger of losing the civil war to al-Qaeda, or a more inclusive Sunni front. Iraq's Shiites are three times as numerous as Iraq's Sunni Arabs; they dominate Iraq's military and police and have a powerful ally in neighboring Iran. The Arab states that might support the Sunnis are small, far away (vast deserts separate the inhabited parts of Jordan and Saudi Arabia from the main Iraqi population centers), and can only provide money, something the insurgency has in great amounts already.

Defeat in Iraq is easy to picture because it has already taken place. Iran's allies dominate Iraq's central government. Iraq is divided along ethnic lines into Arab and Kurdish states and there are civil wars being fought between Sunnis and Shiites in the Arab parts. The United States has no chance of achieving what President Bush has defined as victory: a self-sustaining, democratic, and unified Iraq.

Since at least 2006, George W. Bush has had a very simple Iraq strategy: to run out the clock on his term in office so as to avoid having to admit defeat. On a personal level, the president's denial is understandable. Iraq is the sum of his presidency. To admit failure in Iraq is to admit a failed presidency. (Unlike his fellow Texan, Lyndon Baines Johnson, whose presidency was undone by the Vietnam War, Bush has no "Great Society" to look back on.)

Running out the clock serves George W. Bush's political agenda, and that of his partisans and party. The supposed success of the surge sets up the story line for 2009: After initial difficulties (and perhaps even some mistakes), the United States turned a corner in Iraq in 2007. When George W. Bush left office, America was winning the Iraq War. His successor—abetted by the Democratic Congress and the faithless American people—squandered the victory and is responsible for the consequences.

The pretence that the surge is a success and that therefore

the United States is winning the Iraq War is the opening salvo in a coming blame game as to who lost Iraq. The consequences are not just a matter of partisan politics. The "who lost China" debate of the 1950s ruined the careers of America's top China hands and delayed by a generation a strategically sensible opening to the People's Republic. The finger-pointing over Vietnam poisoned American politics for more than thirty years, delayed by two decades the normalization of relations with Vietnam, and has colored American decision making on key foreign policy questions, including, above all, Iraq.

After Saigon fell to the North Vietnamese army in 1975, the United States simply walked away from Vietnam and all of Indochina. It was not until 1996—twenty-one years later—that President Bill Clinton ended a U.S. trade embargo on Vietnam and restored diplomatic relations. However, the United States does not have the luxury of abandoning Iraq and the Middle East for a generation.

It is therefore a matter of the national interest—and not just partisan interest—that the "Who lost Iraq" debate be settled before George W. Bush leaves office, not afterward. Much that is extremely good has been written about the Iraq fiasco—so much, in fact, that Americans risk losing sight of the main points. Herbert Block, the late cartoonist, once wrote of Richard Nixon that he was the beneficiary of the "Multiple Bad Things Advantage." (Nixon's multiple crimes blurred the public memory of his record so that he eventually died a senior statesman in a way that he might not had he merely committed one single, memorable misdeed.) Similarly, President Bush's Iraq war risked being rescued in part by a public overwhelmed by the pervasiveness of the incompetence. For this reason, it is useful to restate the case as succinctly as possible.

The Iraq War is lost. President Bush and his administration speak of the surge as if victory in Iraq equaled reduced violence and the defeat of al-Qaeda. Before buying into the notion that progress equals victory, it is well to recall Bush's stated objectives for Iraq.

In August 2005, President Bush praised Iraq's new constitution for "its far-reaching protections for fundamental human freedoms, including religion, assembly, conscience, and expression. It vests sovereignty in the people to be expressed by secret ballot and regular elections. It declares that all Iraqis are equal before the law without regard to gender, ethnicity, and religion. This is a document of which the Iraqis and the rest of the world can be proud."

Except in Kurdistan, none of these constitutional provisions apply. There is no freedom of religion in a land where Shiites, Sunnis, Christians, and Yazidis are slaughtered by the thousands because of their faith, including by death squads associated with Iraqi security forces. Freedom of assembly, conscience, and expression exist only on paper, and there is no equality for women, ethnic minorities, or persons from the wrong branch of Islam on the territory of the other branch. There is more freedom in Kurdistan but only because fundamental rights are guaranteed by the draft Kurdistan constitution that is enforced by a virtually independent government.

George W. Bush has defined victory as a unified, democratic, and stable Iraq. Iraq is neither democratic nor unified, and George W. Bush long ago gave up on either goal.

After more than five years of war, George W. Bush will leave office with Baghdad and the southern half of Iraq controlled by Iran's allies and the Sunni center controlled by Baathists. Senator John McCain has accused his Democratic opponent of wanting to surrender in Iraq. But, it is George W. Bush who has already surrendered Iraq to Iran and to the same undemocratic forces that we invaded Iraq to remove.

George W. Bush lost the Iraq War. Much has been written about the mistakes that led to the mess in Iraq. Critics point to the dismissal of the Iraqi army, the draconian de-Baathification decree, and the undue influence of Iraqi opposition leader Ahmad Chalabi. These did not the cause the disaster and the focus on them obscures the larger failure that was the product of incompetence, partisanship, and an obsession with ideology over pragmatism. At the root of the disaster was the absence of presidential decision making. The self-styled decider never decided the most critical questions about the future of Iraq, and worse, never knew there were critical matters that needed deciding. Iraq stands as the great failure of presidential leadership in our time.

Hard as it is to imagine more than five years later, many Iraqis did welcome American troops when they arrived in Baghdad in April 2003. At Firdos square—where Saddam's statue had been toppled five days earlier—an Iraqi man had his grandson pick flowers to give to me. It may be that the underlying tensions in Iraq—the Shiite desire for political power, Sunni resentment over the rise of the Shiites, Kurdish desires for their own state—made victory (defined as a unified, democratic, and stable Iraq) unachievable even at that early stage.

However, two things ensured defeat in the days that followed the U.S. takeover of Iraq: 1) the U.S. failure to stop the looting of Baghdad for weeks after U.S. troops took over the capital; and 2) the decision, made three weeks after U.S. troops were already in Baghdad, to substitute an occupation government for an Iraqi government, and then to put together the occupation government in a slapdash manner with an unquali-fied American administrator at its head and a staff filled with unqualified Republican Party loyalists.

Beginning the day after U.S. troops took over Baghdad, looters attacked and destroyed all but one of Iraq's government ministries. They also robbed banks, shopping centers, and Iraq's cultural institutions, including the Fine Arts Museum, the archaeological museum, and the national library. This loot-ing continued unchecked for at least six weeks. As a result, the United States could not restore essential services (with ministries burned and records destroyed, there was no place for bureaucrats to work) nor jump-start an economy that had sustained billions of dollars in property damage. The looting irretrievably dam-aged American authority. Iraqis thought the Americans would behave in Iraq like the superpower that had crushed Saddam Hussein's army in three weeks and that had shocked and awed Baghdad's defenders with overwhelming, but precisely targeted, fire-power. Instead, the United States showed it was not pre-pared to rule Iraq. In short, the Bush administration showed weakness when it needed to be strong and the U.S. occupation never recovered.

As the looting was taking place, Bush administration of-ficials dismissed it as insignificant. Rumsfeld mocked the net-works for rerunning the footage of a looter stealing a vase and dismissed the destruction of Baghdad as the exuberance of a free people. "Stuff happens," he said. Afterward, however, the Bush administration realized it had a public relations disaster and sought to explain their failure to anticipate and prevent the looting. Douglas J. Feith, the Pentagon official charged with postwar planning faults the CIA. In his memoir *War and Deci-sion* he writes that the CIA predicted that the Iraqi police likely would remain on the job after U.S. troops took Baghdad and that it was unfair to blame the administration when the police did not do as predicted. Paul Wolfowitz, among others, has asserted that the looting was an organized sabotage campaign by Saddam loyalists that the United States could not have prevented. Finally, the administration has argued that the looting was the unfortunate consequence of the success of the agile but small invasion force that ousted Saddam in just three weeks. With a longer war, the United States might have had more troops to maintain order but it would have been at a greater cost in American and Iraqi lives.

All of these arguments are after-the-fact justifications for negligence. The CIA may have stipulated that the Iraqi police stay at their duty stations, but it is the job of military planners—and their civilian overseers—to consider not just the best case but also the less good cases. There were good reasons to expect that the police would not stay on duty when the regime fell. As agents of a repressive regime, the disproportionately Sunni police had reason to fear retribution as well as to wonder how the Americans would view them. At a minimum, any prudent policeman might reasonably be expected to stay at home until events sorted themselves out.

The looting was not organized. I went into at least a dozen government buildings as they were being looted—including the Foreign Ministry, the Trade Ministry, intelligence headquarters, prisons, the former Royal Palace, the Iraqi Olympic Committee, and the residence of Uday Hussein, one of Saddam's sons. In several instances, I went into the buildings alone. In all except Uday's residence, the looters were friendly. They were poor Shiites from Sadr City taking advantage of the complete breakdown in law and order to improve their material position. At the Foreign Ministry, the looters helped my ABC News colleagues find documents, and at the Olympic Committee, they showed us around the burned and looted structure that had once been Uday's fiefdom. I saw no evidence of organized theft and sabotage—and, if it happened at all, it was not common.

The United States could not have prevented all the looting, but it could have protected Iraq's government ministries and most important cultural institutions, even with the relatively small force that first entered Baghdad. In April 2003, the security environment in Baghdad was the least threatening of the entire war. Most ministries and museums were in walled compounds, making them relatively easy to secure.

The United States did not protect Iraq's government ministries and museums because it never occurred to the Bush administration that it had a responsibility to do so. Before the war, the State Department sent the Pentagon a list of fifty sites in Baghdad—including the archaeological museum and government ministries—that should be protected. The list went to the inbox of Undersecretary of Defense Douglas J. Feith, the civilian Rumsfeld designated as responsible for post-war planning, and never came out.

In his memoir, Feith argues that post-war security was the responsibility of General Tommy Franks, the overall theater commander. Franks apparently believed this was Feith's job. The finger-pointing is as irrelevant as it is unseemly.

The President and the Secretary of Defense—not a third-tier Pentagon official or theater commander—should have made sure there was a plan to provide security in Iraq's capital when U.S. forces took it over. The President should have asked the obvious questions: How will security be provided in

Baghdad once U.S. forces take the capital? And, what do we do if the Iraqi police do not stay on the job as we hope? If he asked these questions, he never insisted on answers. This is not a small omission. Because George W. Bush did not insist on planning for the day after Saddam fell, U.S. soldiers have died, billions extra have been spent, and the Iraq war lost.

Famously, during his 2000 campaign, Governor Bush proclaimed, "I don't think our troops ought to be used for what's called nation-building. . . . I think what we need to do is convince people who live in the lands they live in to build the nations. Maybe I'm missing something here. I mean, we're going to have a kind of nation-building corps from America? Absolutely not."

George W. Bush's management of postwar Iraq proved him, at least in this case, to be a man of his word. Because there was no real planning for Iraq's post-invasion governance, the President never made critical decisions about Iraq's future. He did not decide if the Iraqi army would be recalled or dissolved. He never decided whether top Iraqi bureaucrats, almost all of whom were senior members of the Baath party, would be reinstated or fired. And, most critically of all, he never decided how Iraq would be governed after Saddam, and by whom. It was a dereliction of presidential duty without recent precedent made all the more ironic for the fact that President Bush often boasted that his job was to be the decider.

With no decisions having been made before the war, American military and civilian officials arriving in Baghdad in April 2003 began the process of recalling the Iraqi army to its duty stations and of working with senior bureaucrats to get Iraq's looted ministries up and running. Meanwhile, retired Lieutenant General Jay Garner, the man Rumsfeld initially put in charge of Iraq's post-war governance, began the process of consulting with Iraqi politicians about forming an interim Iraqi government. On May 5, Garner announced that the United States would put together the nucleus of an Iraqi government in ten days.

At the end of April, Secretary Rumsfeld appointed retired U.S. diplomat L. Paul (Jerry) Bremer III to replace Garner, making him the Administrator of a newly formed organization called the Coalition Provisional Authority (CPA). The Bush administration pretended the transition from Garner to a Bremer-led CPA was long planned. Bremer, however, explained that he had two weeks between when Rumsfeld asked him to take the assignment and when he showed up in Baghdad. (The American press never made much of this point in spite of both the deceit and incompetence it reflected.) In addition to having no time to prepare, Bremer was by experience and temperament unqualified for the job he now had. Although he had once been a professional diplomat (retired fourteen years at the time he was asked to go to Iraq), Bremer had never served in the Middle East, had never been to Iraq, and had never served in a post-conflict society. As an administrator, he was a control freak whose arrogance put off all the Iraqis with whom he dealt, contributing to his ineffectiveness. (Only one of the many Iraqi leaders with whom Bremer worked closely had a kind word to say about him. The exception was a Kurdish leader who told me he wanted to erect a statue of Bremer since "he had done more to break up Iraq than anyone else.")

Within days after arriving in Baghdad, Bremer reversed the decisions Garner and his team had taken just a few weeks before. In his first order, he issued a decree banning members of the top four ranks of the Baath party from public service, in effect firing all the country's experienced bureaucrats at a time when their skills were most needed. In his second decree, Bremer dissolved the Iraqi Army and security services, making enemies of hundreds of thousands of newly unemployed, and well-armed, young men. He told Iraq's political leaders that there would be no interim government and that he would run the country for an indefinite period of time. Although these decisions were hugely consequential, they never went to Bush. Rumsfeld, Bremer's nominal superior, has said he was not consulted on either the decision to dissolve the Iraqi Army or on the de-Baathification decree. According to Feith, George Bush had approved a Defense Department plan to avoid a prolonged military occupation by launching a new Iraqi government but that the plan was buried by policy disputes among senior officials. These three decisions—to dissolve the Iraqi army, to fire Baathist bureaucrats, and to have a prolonged United States–run occupation of Iraq—were the most momentous of Bush's presidency, and the President never made them. And, if Feith is to be believed, Bush decided against a prolonged occupation of Iraq but was too weak or too inattentive to make his own administration follow his orders.

Four months later, as the insurgency was gathering steam, Bremer published an op-ed in the *Washington Post* in which he laid out a scenario for a transition from U.S. occupation to Iraqi rule that was so complicated that it would have taken years to implement. No one in the Bush administration ever saw— much less reviewed—Bremer's transition plan. George W. Bush unknowingly delegated authority for the most important project of his administration to a neophyte.

Bremer defends his decisions on the dissolving the army and barring Baathists from public service by saying these were the most popular actions he took as Iraq's administrator. Bremer's critics rarely take this point seriously, but it is very relevant. Saddam's army was a Sunni-run institution in a Shiite-majority state. It committed genocide against the Kurds in the 1980s, suppressed the Shiite uprising in 1991, and carried out the genocide against the Marsh Arabs in the 1990s. This army could not have co-existed in an Iraq now run by Shiites and Kurds. Similarly, it is hard to imagine that Iraq's Shiite and Kurdish ministers would have trusted bureaucrats from a party that had repressed them and, in the case of the Kurds, sought to exterminate them.

Nonetheless, Bremer's high-handedness created unnecessary enemies. Since Saddam's army had already vanished (as Bremer explained later to justify his decree), there was no need to dissolve it. Sunni officers saw the decree as insulting and arrogant, and there is no doubt that the decree—not just the fact of not recalling the army—added to Sunni bitterness and helped drive men with weapons, and knowledge of how to use them, to the insurgency. The de-Baathification order was both too extreme and interfered with the urgent short-term goal of reconstituting Iraq's bureaucracy. Almost all of Iraq's top civil servants were members of the Baath party and therefore were banned from their old positions. As a result, from mid-May 2003, not only were Iraq's government offices largely empty shells without files and furniture but the experienced managers had all been fired. The decree also affected tens of thousands of others, including teachers and doctors, who joined the Baath party simply to advance their careers.

The main problem with Bremer's decrees is that he issued them. Firing Iraq's Sunni-led army and bureaucracy was probably inevitable, but it should have been done by an Iraqi government and not ostentatiously by an American pro-consul. The controversy over the firings has all but obscured an even larger error—how Bremer and the Bush administration replaced the fired soldiers and bureaucrats.

To fill vacancies in ministries and in local governments, CPA turned to Iraq's political parties. The Shiite religious parties became major beneficiaries of U.S. patronage, consolidating their control of the South and putting cadres into central government ministries. The CPA also allowed the Shiite religious parties to place their militiamen into Iraq's newly constituted security forces.

Nominally, the new Iraqi Army had Shiite, Sunni, and Kurdish battalions (only one of 115 battalions was mixed in 2005). The Sunni battalions, however, existed only on paper, and the Kurdish battalions were peshmerga loyal to the Kurdistan chain of command. The new army was—and is—effectively a Shiite army. Many of its officers and recruits came from the militia associated with the Shiite religious parties, the most important of which were recruited and trained by Iran. Thus, Bremer effectively transformed the Iraqi Army from a Sunni institution that was the bulwark against Iran to a Shiite institution allied with—and infiltrated by—Iran. When the Shiite religious parties won parliamentary elections in January 2005, they accelerated the process of making Iraq into a Shiite religious state that Bremer had started.

Bremer's occupation government lasted fourteen months and accomplished almost nothing. Under Bremer's watch, oil and electricity production plummeted. Unemployment rose sharply, and security deteriorated. Bremer did issue a lot of decrees—one hundred in total. Some were pet conservative projects—a 15 percent flat income tax in a country where no one paid taxes—while others dealt with more practical issues such as control of borders. Some were part of a larger scheme to revamp Iraqi society by privatizing basic industries and creating new institutions. Almost none had any practical effect.

Bremer and his team devoted considerable effort to writing an interim Iraqi constitution that President Bush proclaimed to be among the most liberal and democratic in the Middle East. But, like almost everything the CPA attempted, it did not apply beyond the fortified Green Zone, where the American occupation government had its seat. In the south, Shiite religious parties ignored the interim constitution's human rights provisions to establish their theocracies, and the CPA, which had representatives in "mini Green Zones" in the principal cities in the south, did nothing to stop this. In visits to Kurdistan, Bremer lectured the Kurds on being part of the new Iraq. They listened politely, told him what he wanted to hear, and then strengthened their separate state. The CPA never established its authority in Baghdad or the Sunni center; within months, the Sunni insurgency had made these areas too dangerous.

Fantasy government is one reason the CPA was so ineffective. But another major factor is that so many of its key personnel had no qualifications for the jobs they held. Rather than recruit professionals to help make Iraq a success, the Bush administration treated positions in the CPA as patronage for Republicans and conservative activists. Frederick Burkle, a medical doctor with vast experience in supporting health-care systems after conflicts, was hired before the war to help reestablish the Iraqi system. After a few weeks on the job, he was replaced by a Michigan Republican who was not a medical doctor and whose international experience consisted of a few trips abroad. Six twenty-somethings, recruited via the Web site of the Heritage

Foundation, a conservation Washington think tank, were put in charge of spending Iraq's $13 billion budget. Having no relevant qualifications (one had not even finished college), they failed to spend more than a few hundred million dollars. Putting unqualified people into important positions meant that spending that could have created jobs to stimulate the economy did not take place and that medical care was not provided.

The Bush administration was promiscuous in permitting conservative activists to go to Iraq, and even design their own projects. Young Republicans created a new set of traffic laws and set up a high-tech Baghdad stock exchange (unfortunately without many stocks to be traded). At one meeting of the senior staff, two young men in dark suits appeared, and after some evasion, explained they were from the FBI. Burkle, who had yet to be replaced, demanded to know why the FBI was in the meeting. The young men explained they were there to convert Iraqis to Christianity. Only then did Burkle understand that FBI stood for the White House's Faith-Based Initiative.*

At a February 6, 2007, hearing of the House Committee on Oversight and Government Reform, Democrats questioned Bremer about the unqualified people sent to Iraq. He replied that Foreign Service officers served in CPA, including in some of his key deputy slots. This misses the point. The presence of qualified professionals in the CPA does not excuse or mitigate the consequences of having unqualified patronage

---

* This story is not recounted to suggest that the administration ever considered trying to convert Iraqis, which obviously it did not. The anecdote is only meant to illustrate how ill disciplined the Bush administration was in choosing people to send to the war zone.

appointees in a mission of such sensitivity and importance. The failure to create jobs or to provide health care infuriated Iraqis and, among the Sunnis and Shiite poor, created a pool of idle and angry men, some of whom joined the Sunni insurgency or the Shiites' Mahdi Army. CPA's failures—due in part to the nature of its staffing—destroyed any chance of success in Iraq and, by helping fuel the anger that fed the insurgency, contributed to the deaths of American servicemen and women.

The Bush administration's main mistake was the occupation itself. Any Iraqi government would have done a better job than the hapless Coalition Provisional Authority. In the run-up to war, President Bush and his top officials attached great importance to the arguments for war advanced by Iraqi exiles, and in particular to those of Ahmad Chalabi. After taking Baghdad, the Bush administration abruptly decided that these same exiles were unfit to run Iraq. Instead, the United States would run the country until power could be handed over to a more representative group of Iraqis. When elections were finally held in January 2005, the supposedly unrepresentative exiles (along with the Kurds) won 90 percent of the vote.

In spite of being away for decades, Ahmad Chalabi and his fellow exiles understood Iraq far better than the amateurs the Bush administration sent to the country. President Bush clearly would have done better to have stuck to his original plan—if Feith is right that this most disengaged of presidents had approved a plan—and installed an Iraqi interim government from the start. As conceived by the Iraqi opposition groups and General Garner, such a government would have been a coalition of secular Arab Iraqis, Shiite religious parties, and Kurdish nationalist parties. Such a government would have had popular

support. In the January 2005, the United Iraqi Alliance, a coalition of Shiite religious parties led by SCIRI and Dawa (and
some secular Shiites) won more than 50 percent of the vote.
Massoud Barzani's Kurdistan Democratic Party (KDP) and Jalal
Talabani's Patriotic Union of Kurdistan (PUK) ran together as a
slate and won a quarter of the vote. Because the Sunnis so vehemently opposed a Shiite-led Iraq, no interim Iraqi government
could have effectively represented them, although it certainly
would have included Sunnis. This inability to include representative Sunnis was one major argument against forming an
interim government. The CPA, however, was equally unable to
reach out to Sunnis.

Ahmad Chalabi might well have become Iraq's prime minister or president but he would have been responsible to Shiite and Kurdish politicians more powerful than he was. Bush's
critics blame much of the Iraq disaster on Chalabi, whom they
portray as a crook who conned the administration into an ill-
advised war with false information about Saddam's WMD and
visions of Iraqis greeting their American liberators with flowers
and sweets. Having known Chalabi for more than twenty years,
I think this caricature has done a disservice to him and to the
United States. Chalabi has proved himself to be a brilliant strategist. He wanted to get to rid of Saddam and, lacking his own
army, persuaded the United States to have its army do what he
wanted. Had the CIA been able to do what Chalabi did—get
a foreign power to spend hundreds of billions of dollars to accomplish U.S. foreign policy goals—it would be described as
the most brilliant psychological operation ever. Someone able
to get the United States to invade Iraq—especially when Iraq
posed no threat to the United States—is a very capable human

being and, given a chance, might have done a respectable job running Iraq. He could not have done a worse job than CPA.

Having a Shiite-Kurdish interim government instead of a U.S. occupation probably would not have prevented the Sunni insurgency. With their knowledge of the country, a Shiite-Kurdish government might have more effectively countered it than the clueless U.S. occupation regime. In 2003, Moqtada al-Sadr's movement was small, and it might have stayed that way if the Shiites—and not the Americans—had been governing Iraq. Most importantly, a bona fide Iraqi government led by a secular Iraqi like Chalabi might have limited the influence and political power of the Shiite religious parties and therefore of Iran.

Whether an interim Iraqi government led by Shiites and Kurds actually would have contained the insurgency or limited the power of the religious Shiite parties and movements is, as Secretary Rumsfeld might have put it, a known unknown. Such a government would have had the virtue of representing 80 percent of the Iraqi people. And that would have been a lot better than Bremer and his team who represented—and served— no one.

Because President Bush never decided the important issues, it is hard to pinpoint how and where the administration veered from its initial plan for an interim Iraqi Government into an American occupation. But clearly this issue was caught in the struggle over foreign policy between the professionals, led by Secretary of State Colin Powell and Director of Central Intelligence George Tenet, and the ideologues as represented by Vice President Dick Cheney, Paul Wolfowitz, Douglas Feith, and Cheney's staff. Rumsfeld may have been less ideological than his subordinates but generally supported them. Having lost the main battle on whether to go to war, the professionals exacted retribution on the ideologues by undermining their man Chalabi and with him the idea of an interim Iraqi Government. Since neither Bush nor Rumsfeld felt strongly about Chalabi (unlike their subordinates), this was a battle the professionals could win. But, having blocked Chalabi, and with him the idea of an interim government, Powell and Tenet had nothing else to offer. A disastrous occupation government became the default option.

A stronger president would have personally considered all the options for Iraq's post-war governance and then, well in advance of an invasion, made his decisions. A strong president would never have tolerated the level of infighting and insubordination that took place within the Bush Administration on Iraq.

It may be that the goal of a unified, democratic, and stable Iraq was never attainable. If so, George W. Bush sent U.S. troops into harm's way with an impossible mission.

But if there had ever been a chance for success, George W. Bush's weak leadership guaranteed failure. Bush did not insist on a workable plan to provide security in Baghdad, and, as best I can tell, never even considered the matter. He did not make a timely or clear decision on what turned out to be the most critical question of his presidency, that is, how Iraq would be ruled after the invasion. From the day U.S. troops seized Baghdad, it took three weeks for his administration to choose an American administrator for Iraq, and it then chose a man unqualified by experience and temperament. Bush allowed the Coalition Provisional Authority to be a playground for his fellow Republicans while U.S. troops risked their lives trying to carry out an unplanned occupation. He never noticed as his Iraq team installed Iran's allies in key positions in the Iraqi government, in the oil-rich southern provinces, and in the new Iraqi Army. He never realized that the Iraq War planning was, for the most part, best-case analysis and that his job was not just to decide but also to question.

George W. Bush lost Iraq.

3

The Victor

In his continuing effort to bolster support for the Iraq War, President Bush traveled to Reno, Nevada, on August 28, 2007, to speak to the annual convention of the American Legion. He emphatically warned of the Iranian threat should the United States withdraw from Iraq. Said the president, "For all those who ask whether the fight in Iraq is worth it, imagine an Iraq where militia groups backed by Iran control large parts of the country."

On the same day, in the southern Iraqi city of Karbala, the Mahdi Army, a militia loyal to the radical Shiite cleric Moqtada al-Sadr, battled government security forces around the shrine of Imam Hussein, one of Shiite Islam's holiest places. A million pilgrims were in the city and fifty-one died.

The United States did not directly intervene, but American jets flew overhead in support of the government security forces. As elsewhere in the south, those Iraqi forces are dominated by the Badr Organization, a militia founded, trained, armed, and financed by Iran. When U.S. forces ousted Saddam's regime from the south in early April 2003, the Badr Organization infiltrated from Iran to fill the void left by the Bush administration's failure to plan for security and governance in postinvasion Iraq.

In the months that followed, the U.S.-run Coalition Provisional Authority (CPA) appointed Badr Organization leaders to key positions in Iraq's American-created army and police. At the same time, L. Paul Bremer's CPA appointed party officials from the Supreme Council for the Islamic Revolution in Iraq (SCIRI) to be governors and serve on governorate councils throughout southern Iraq. As noted earlier, SCIRI, (now SIIC), was founded at the Ayatollah Khomeini's direction in Tehran in 1982. The Badr Organization is the militia associated with SCIRI.

In the January 2005 elections, SCIRI became the most important component of Iraq's ruling Shiite coalition. In exchange for not taking the prime minister's slot, SCIRI won the right to name key ministers, including the minister of the interior. From that ministry, SCIRI placed Badr militiamen throughout Iraq's national police.

In short, George W. Bush had from the first facilitated the very event he warned would be a disastrous consequence of a U.S. withdrawal from Iraq: the takeover of a large part of the country by an Iranian-backed militia. And while the president contrasts the promise of democracy in Iraq with the tyranny in Iran, there is now substantially more personal freedom in Iran than in southern Iraq.

Iran's role in Iraq is pervasive, but also subtle. When Iraq drafted its permanent constitution in 2005, the American ambassador energetically engaged in all parts of the process. But behind the scenes, the Iranian ambassador intervened to block provisions that Tehran did not like. As it happened, both the Americans and the Iranians wanted to strengthen Iraq's central government. While the Bush administration clung to the mirage of a single Iraqi people, Tehran worked to give its proxies, the pro-Iranian Iraqis it supported—by then established as the government of Iraq—as much power as possible. (Thanks to Kurdish obstinacy, neither the United States nor Iran succeeded in its goal, but even now both countries want to see the central government strengthened.)

Since 2005, Iraq's Shiite-led government has concluded numerous economic, political, and military agreements with Iran. The most important would link the two countries' strategic oil reserves by building a pipeline from southern Iraq to Iran, while another commits Iran to providing extensive military assistance to the Iraqi government. According to a senior official in Iraq's Oil Ministry, smugglers in 2007 diverted at least 150,000 barrels of Iraq's daily oil exports through Iran, a figure that approached 10 percent of Iraq's production. Iran has yet to provide the military support it promised to the Iraqi Army. With the United States supplying 160,000 troops and hundreds of billions of dollars to support a pro-Iranian Iraqi government, Iran has no reason to invest its own resources.

Of all the unintended consequences of the Iraq War, Iran's strategic victory is the most far-reaching. In establishing the border between the Ottoman Empire and the Persian Empire in 1639, the Treaty of Qasr-i-Shirin demarcated the boundary between Sunni-ruled lands and Shiite-ruled lands. For eight years of brutal warfare in the 1980s, Iran tried to breach that line but could not. (At the time, the Reagan administration supported

Saddam Hussein precisely because it feared the strategic consequences of an Iraq dominated by Iran's allies.) The U.S. invasion of Iraq in 2003 accomplished what Khomeini's army could
not. Today, the Shiite-controlled lands extend to the borders
of Kuwait and Saudi Arabia. Bahrain, a Persian Gulf kingdom
with a Shiite majority and a Sunni monarch, is most affected by
these developments, but so is Saudi Arabia's Eastern Province,
which is home to most of the kingdom's Shiites. (They may
even be a majority in the province but this is unknown since
Saudi Arabia has not dared to conduct a census.) The U.S. Navy
has its most important Persian Gulf base in Bahrain while most
of Saudi Arabia's oil is under the Eastern Province.

America's Iraq quagmire has given new life to Iran's Syrian
ally, Bashir Assad. In 2003, the Syrian Baathist regime seemed
an anachronism unable to survive the region's political and economic changes. Today, Assad appears firmly in control, having
even recovered from the opprobrium of having his regime implicated in the assassination of former Lebanese prime minister
Rafik Hariri. In Lebanon, Hezbollah enjoys greatly enhanced
stature for having held off the Israelis in the 2006 war. As Hezbollah's sponsor and source of arms, Iran now has an influence
both in the Levant and in the Arab-Israeli conflict that it never
before had.

The scale of the American miscalculation is striking. Before the Iraq War began, its neoconservative architects argued
that conferring power on Iraq's Shiites would serve to *undermine* Iran because Iraq's Shiites, controlling the faith's two holiest cities, would, in the words of then deputy defense secretary
Paul Wolfowitz, be "an independent source of authority for the
Shia religion emerging in a country that is democratic and pro-
Western." Furthermore they argued, Iran could never dominate

Iraq, because the Iraqi Shiites are Arabs and the Iranian Shiites are Persian. It was a theory that, unfortunately, had no connection to reality.

Iran's bond with the Iraqi Shiites goes far beyond the support Iran gave Shiite leaders in their struggle with Saddam Hussein. Decades of oppression have made their religious identity more important to Iraqi Shiites than their Arab ethnic identity. (Also, many Iraqi Shiites have Turkmen, Persian, or Kurdish ancestors.) While Sunnis identify with the Arab world, Iraqi Shiites identify with the Shiite world, and for many this means Iran.

There is also the legacy of February 15, 1991, when President George H. W. Bush called on the Iraqi people to rise up against Saddam Hussein. Two weeks later, the Shiites in southern Iraq did just that. When Saddam's Republican Guards moved south to crush the rebellion, President Bush went fishing and no help was given. Only Iran showed sympathy. Hundreds of thousands died and no Iraqi Shiite I know thinks this failure of U.S. support was anything but intentional. In assessing the loyalty of the Iraqi Shiites before the war, the war's architects often stressed how Iraqi Shiite conscripts fought loyally for Iraq in the Iran-Iraq War. They never mentioned the 1991 betrayal. This was understandable: at the end of the 1991 war, Wolfowitz was the number three man at the Pentagon, Dick Cheney was the defense secretary, and, of course, Bush's father was the president.

Iran and its Iraqi allies control, respectively, the Middle East's third- and second-largest oil reserves. Iran's influence now extends to the borders of the Saudi province that holds the world's largest oil reserves. President Bush has responded to these strategic changes wrought by his own policies by strongly supporting a pro-Iranian government in Baghdad and by arming and training the most pro-Iranian elements in the Iraqi military and police.

Beginning with his 2002 State of the Union speech, President Bush has articulated two main U.S. goals for Iran: 1) the replacement of Iran's theocratic regime with a liberal democracy and 2) preventing Iran from acquiring nuclear weapons. Since events in Iraq took a bad turn, he has added a third objective: gaining Iranian cooperation in Iraq.

The administration's track record is not impressive. The prospects for liberal democracy in Iran took a severe blow when reform-minded president Mohammad Khatami was replaced by the hard-line—and somewhat erratic—Mahmoud Ahmadinejad in August 2005. (Khatami had won two landslide elections that were a vote to soften the ruling theocracy; after taking office, he was prevented by the conservative clerics from accomplishing much.) At the time President Bush first proclaimed his intention to keep nuclear weapons out of Iranian hands, Iran had no means of making fissile material. Since then, however, Iran has defied the IAEA and the U.N. Security Council to assemble and use the centrifuges needed to enrich uranium. In Iraq, the administration accuses Iran of supplying particularly potent roadside bombs to Shiite militias *and* Sunni insurgents.

To coerce Iran into ceasing its uranium enrichment program, the Bush administration has relied on U.N. sanctions, the efforts of a European negotiating team, and stern presidential warnings. The mismanaged Iraq War has undercut all these efforts. After seeing the United States go to the United Nations with allegedly irrefutable evidence that Iraq possessed chemical and biological weapons and had a covert nuclear program, foreign governments and publics are understandably skeptical about the veracity of Bush administration statements on Iran. The Iraq experience makes many countries reluctant to support meaningful sanctions not only because they doubt administration statements but because they are afraid President Bush will interpret any Security Council resolution condemning Iran as an authorization for war.

With so much of the U.S. military tied up in Iraq, the Iranians do not believe America has the resources to attack them and then deal with the consequences. They know that an attack on Iran would have little support in the United States—it is doubtful that Congress would authorize it—and none internationally. Not even the British would go along with a military strike on Iran. President Bush's warnings count for little with Tehran because he now has a long record of tough language unmatched by action. As long as the Iranians believe the United States has no military option, they have limited incentives to reach an agreement, especially with the Europeans.

The administration's efforts to change Iran's regime have been feeble or feckless. President Bush's freedom rhetoric is supported by Radio Farda, a U.S.-sponsored Persian language radio station, and a $75 million appropriation to finance Iranian opposition activities including satellite broadcasts by Los Angeles–based exiles. If only regime change were so easily accomplished!

The identity of Iranian recipients of U.S. funding is secret, but the administration's neoconservative allies have loudly promoted American military and financial support for Iranian opposition groups as diverse as the son of the late Shah, Iranian Kurdish separatists, and the Mujahedin-e Khalq (MEK), which is on the State Department's list of terrorist organizations. Some of the Los Angeles exiles now being funded are associated with the son of the Shah, but it is unlikely that either the MEK or the Kurdish separatists have received any of the $75 million. Nonetheless, U.S. secrecy and the fact that the administration treats the MEK differently from other terrorist organizations has roused Iranian suspicions that the United States is supporting these groups either through the democracy program or a separate covert action.

None of these groups is a plausible agent for regime change. The Shah's son is identified with a corrupt and discredited monarchy. Iranian Kurdistan is seething with discontent, and Iranian security forces have suppressed large antiregime demonstrations there. Kurdish nationalism on the margins of Iran, however, does not weaken the Iranian regime at the center. (While the U.S. State Department has placed the PKK, a Kurdish rebel movement in Turkey, on its list of terrorist organizations, PEJAK, the PKK's Iranian branch, is not on the list and its leaders even visit the United States.)

The Mujahedin-e Khalq is one of the oldest—and nastiest—of the Iranian opposition groups. After originally supporting the Iranian revolution, the MEK broke with Khomeini and relocated to Iraq in the early stages of the Iran-Iraq War. It was so closely connected to Saddam that MEK fighters not only assisted the Iraqis in the Iran-Iraq War but also helped Saddam put down the 1991 Kurdish uprising. While claiming to be democratic and pro-Western, the MEK closely resembles a cult. In April 2003, when I visited Camp Ashraf, its main base, northeast of Baghdad, I found robotlike hero worship of the MEK's leaders, Massoud and Maryam Rajavi. The fighters I met parroted a revolutionary party line, and there were transparently crude efforts at propaganda. To emphasize its being a modern organization as distinct from the Tehran theocrats, the MEK appointed a woman as Camp Ashraf's nominal commander and maintained a women's tank battalion. The commander was clearly not in command and the women mechanics supposedly working on tank engines all had spotless uniforms.

Both the State Department and Iran consider the MEK to be terrorist group. The U.S. government, however, does not always act as if the MEK were one. During the 2003 invasion of Iraq, the U.S. military dropped a single bomb on Camp Ashraf. It struck the women's barracks at a time of day when the soldiers were not there. When I visited two weeks later with an ABC camera crew, we filmed the MEK bringing a scavenged Iraqi tank into their base. U.S. forces drove in and out of Camp Ashraf, making no effort to detain the supposed terrorists or to stop them from collecting Iraqi heavy weapons. Since Iran had its agents in Iraq from the time Saddam fell (and may have been doing its own scavenging of weapons), one can presume that this behavior did not go unnoticed. Subsequently, the U.S. military did disarm the MEK, but in spite of hostility from both the Shiites and Kurds, who now jointly dominate Iraq's government, its fighters are still at Camp Ashraf. Rightly or wrongly, many Iranians conclude from this that the United States is supporting a terrorist organization that is fomenting violence inside Iran.

Halting Iran's nuclear program and changing its regime are incompatible objectives. Iran is highly unlikely to agree to a negotiated solution with the United States (or the Europeans) while the Americans are trying to overthrow its government. Air strikes may destroy Iran's nuclear facilities but they will rally popular support for the regime and give it a fresh pretext to crack down on the opposition.

From the perspective of U.S. national security strategy, the choice should be easy. Iran's most prominent democrats have stated publicly that they do not want U.S. support. In a 2007 open letter to U.N. Secretary-General Ban Ki-moon, the Iranian dissident Akbar Ganji criticized both the Iranian regime and U.S. hypocrisy. "Far from helping the development of democracy," he wrote, "US policy over the past 50 years has consistently been to the detriment of the proponents of freedom and democracy in Iran. . . . The Bush Administration, for its part, by approving a fund for democracy assistance in Iran, which is in fact being largely spent on official institutions and media affiliated with the US government, has made it easy for the Iranian regime to describe its opponents as mercenaries of the US and to crush them with impunity."

Even though they can't accomplish it, Bush administration leaders have been unwilling to abandon regime change in Iran as a goal. Its advocates compare their efforts to the support the United States gave democrats behind the Iron Curtain over many decades. But there is a crucial difference. The Soviet and Eastern European dissidents wanted U.S. support, which was sometimes personally costly but politically welcome. But this is immaterial to administration ideologues. They are, to borrow Jeane Kirkpatrick's phrase, deeply committed to policies that feel good rather than do good. If Congress wants to help the Iranian opposition, it should cut off funding for Iranian democracy programs.

Right now, the United States is in the worst possible position. It is identified with the most discredited part of the Iranian opposition and unwanted by the reformers who have the most appeal to Iranians. Many Iranians believe that the United States is fomenting violence inside their country, and this becomes a pretext for attacks on American troops in Iraq. And for its pains, the U.S. accomplishes nothing.

For eighteen years, Iran had a secret program aimed at acquiring the technology that could make nuclear weapons. A. Q. Khan, the supposedly rogue leader of Pakistan's Atomic Energy Commission, provided centrifuges to enrich uranium and bomb designs. After the Khan network was exposed, Iran declared in October 2003 its enrichment program to the International Atomic Energy Agency (IAEA), provided an accounting (perhaps not complete) of its nuclear activities, and agreed to suspend its uranium enrichment. Following the election of Ahmadinejad as president in 2005, Iran announced it would resume its uranium enrichment activities. During the last three years, it has assembled cascades of centrifuges and apparently enriched a small amount of uranium to the 5 percent level required for certain types of nuclear power reactors (weapons require 80 to 90 percent enrichment but this is not technically very difficult once the initial enrichment processes are mastered).

The United States has two options for dealing with Iran's nuclear facilities: military strikes to destroy them or negotiations to neutralize them. The first is risky and the second may not produce results. The Bush administration has not pursued either option, preferring U.N. sanctions (which, so far, have been more symbolic than punitive) and relying on Europeans to take the lead in negotiations. But neither sanctions nor the European initiative is likely to work. As long as Iran's primary concern is the United States, it is unlikely to settle for a deal that involves only Europe.

Sustained air strikes probably could halt Iran's nuclear program. While some Iranian facilities may be hidden and others protected deep underground, the locations of major facilities are known. Even if it is not possible to destroy all the facilities, Iran's scientists, engineers, and construction crews are unlikely to show up for work at places that are subject to ongoing bombing.

But the risks from air strikes are great. Many of the potential targets are in populated places, endangering civilians both from errant bombs and the possible dispersal of radioactive material. The rest of the world would condemn the attacks and there would likely be a virulent anti-American reaction in the Islamic world. In retaliation, Iran could wreak havoc on the world economy (and its own) by withholding oil from the global market and by military action to close the Persian Gulf shipping lanes.

The main risk to the United States comes in Iraq. Faced with choosing between the Americans and Iran, Iraq's government may not choose its liberator. And even if the Iraqi government did not openly cooperate with the Iranians, pro-Iranian elements in the U.S.-armed military and police almost certainly would facilitate attacks on American troops by pro-Iranian Iraqi militia or by Iranian forces infiltrated across Iraq's porous border. A few days after Bush's August 28 speech, Iranian general Rahim Yahya Safavi underscored Iran's ability to retaliate, saying of U.S. troops in the region, "We have accurately identified all their camps." Unless he chooses to act with reckless disregard for the safety of U.S. troops in Iraq, President Bush has effectively denied himself a military option for dealing with the Iranian nuclear program.

A diplomatic solution to the crisis created by Iran's nuclear program is clearly preferable, but not necessarily achievable. Broadly speaking, states want nuclear weapons for two reasons: security and prestige. Under the Shah, Iran had a nuclear program but Khomeini disbanded it after the 1979 revolution on the grounds that nuclear weapons were un-Islamic. When the program resumed covertly in the mid-1980s, Iran's primary security concern was Iraq. At that time, Iraq had its own covert nuclear program; more immediately, it had threatened Iran with chemical weapons attacks on its cities. An Iranian nuclear weapon could serve as a deterrent to both Iraqi chemical and nuclear weapons.

With Iraq's defeat in the Persian Gulf War, the Iraqi threat greatly diminished. And of course it vanished after Iran's allies took power in Baghdad after the 2003 invasion. Today, Iran sees the United States as the main threat to its security. American military forces surround Iran—in Afghanistan, Iraq, Central Asia, and on the Persian Gulf. President Bush and his top aides repeatedly express solidarity with the Iranian people against their government while the United States finances programs aimed at the government's ouster. The American and international press are full of speculation that Vice President Cheney wants Bush to attack Iran before his term ends. From an Iranian perspective, all this smoke could indicate a fire.

In 2003, there was enough common ground for a deal. In May 2003, the Iranian authorities sent a proposal through the Swiss ambassador in Tehran, Tim Guldimann, for negotiations on a package deal in which Iran would freeze its nuclear program in exchange for an end to U.S. hostility. The Iranian paper offered "full transparency for security that there are no Iranian endeavors to develop or possess WMD [and] full cooperation with the IAEA based on Iranian adoption of all relevant instruments." The Iranians also offered support for "the establishment of democratic institutions and a non-religious government" in Iraq; full cooperation against terrorists (including "above all, al-

Qaeda"); and an end to material support to Palestinian groups such as Hamas. In return, the Iranians asked that their country not be on the terrorism list or designated part of the "Axis of Evil"; that all sanctions end; that the United States support Iran's claims for reparations for the Iran-Iraq War as part of the overall settlement of the Iraqi debt; that they have access to peaceful nuclear technology; and that the United States pursue anti-Iranian terrorists, including "above all" the MEK. MEK members should, the Iranians said, be repatriated to Iran.

Basking in the glory of "Mission Accomplished" in Iraq, the Bush administration dismissed the Iranian offer and criticized Guldimann for even presenting it. Several years later, the Bush administration's abrupt rejection of the Iranian offer began to look blatantly foolish and the administration moved to suppress the story. Flynt Leverett, who had handled Iran in 2003 for the National Security Council, tried to write about it in the *New York Times* and found his op-ed crudely censored by the NSC, which had to clear it. Guldimann, however, had given the Iranian paper to Ohio Republican congressman Bob Ney, now remembered both for renaming House cafeteria food and for larceny. (As chairman of the House Administration Committee he renamed French fries "freedom fries" and is now in federal prison for bribery.) I was surprised to learn that Ney had a serious side. He had lived in Iran before the revolution, spoke Farsi, and wanted better relations between the two countries. Trita Parsi, Ney's staffer in 2003, describes in detail the Iranian offer and the Bush administration's high-handed rejection of it in his informative account of the triangular relationship among the United States, Iran, and Israel, *Treacherous Alliance: The Secret Dealings of Israel, Iran, and the United States.*

Four years later, Iran holds a much stronger hand while the

mismanagement of the Iraq occupation has made the U.S. position incomparably weaker. While the 2003 proposal could not have been presented without support from the clerics who really run Iran, Iran's current president, Mahmoud Ahmadinejad, has made uranium enrichment the centerpiece of his administration and the embodiment of Iranian nationalism. Even though Ahmadinejad does not make decisions about Iran's nuclear program (and his finger would never be on the button if Iran had a bomb), he has made it politically very difficult for the clerics to come back to the 2003 paper.

Nonetheless, the 2003 Iranian paper could provide a starting point for a U.S.-Iran deal. In recent years, various ideas have emerged that could accommodate both Iran's insistence on its right to nuclear technology and the international community's desire for ironclad assurances that Iran will not divert the technology into weapons. These include a Russian proposal that Iran enrich uranium on Russian territory and an idea floated by U.S. and Iranian experts to have a European consortium conduct the enrichment in Iran under international supervision. Iran rejected the Russian proposal, but if hostility between Iran and United States were to be reduced, it might be revived. (The consortium idea has no official standing at this point.) While there are good reasons to doubt Iranian statements that its program is entirely peaceful, Iran remains a party to the Nuclear Non-Proliferation Treaty and its leaders, including Ahmadinejad, insist it has no intention of developing nuclear weapons. As long as this is the case, Iran could make a deal to limit its nuclear program without losing face.

From the inception of Iran's nuclear program under the Shah, prestige and the desire for recognition have been motivating factors. Iranians want the world, and especially the United

States, to see Iran as they do themselves—as a populous, powerful, and responsible country that is heir to a great empire and home to a 2,500-year-old civilization. In Iranian eyes, the United States has behaved in a way that continually diminishes their country. Many Iranians still seethe over the U.S. involvement in the 1953 coup that overthrew the government of democratically elected prime minister Mohammad Mossadegh and reinstated the Shah. Being designated a terrorist state and part of an "Axis of Evil" grates on the Iranians in the same way. In some ways, the 1979–81 hostage crisis and Iran's nuclear program were different strategies to compel U.S. respect for Iran. A diplomatic overture toward Iran might include ways to show respect for Iranian civilization (which is different from approval of its leaders) and could include an open apology for the U.S. role in the 1953 coup, which, as it turned out, was a horrible mistake for U.S. interests.

While President Bush insists that time is not on America's side, the process of negotiation—and even an interim agreement—might provide time for more moderate Iranians to assert themselves. So far as Iran's security is concerned, possession of nuclear weapons is more a liability than an asset. Iran's size—and the certainty of strong resistance—is sufficient deterrent to any U.S. invasion, which, even at the height of the Bush administration's post-Saddam euphoria, was never seriously considered. Developing nuclear weapons would provide Iran with no additional deterrent to a U.S. invasion but could invite an attack.

Should al-Qaeda or another terrorist organization succeed in detonating a nuclear weapon in an American city, any U.S. president would look to the country that supplied the weapon as a place to retaliate. If the origin of the bomb were unknown, a nuclear Iran—a designated state sponsor of terrorism—would find itself a likely target, even though it is extremely unlikely to supply such a weapon to al-Qaeda, a Sunni fundamentalist organization. With its allies now largely running the government in Baghdad, Iran does not need a nuclear weapon to deter a hostile Iraq. An Iranian bomb, however, likely would cause Saudi Arabia to acquire nuclear weapons, thus canceling Iran's considerable manpower advantage over its Gulf rival. More pragmatic leaders, such as former president Akbar Hashemi Rafsanjani, may understand this. Rafsanjani, who lost the 2005 presidential elections to Ahmadinejad, is making a comeback, defeating a hard-liner to become chairman of Iran's Assembly of Experts for the Leadership (Majles-e Khobrgran Rahbari), which appoints and can dismiss the supreme leader.

At this stage, neither the United States nor Iran seems willing to talk directly about bilateral issues apart from Iraq. Even if the two sides did talk, there is no guarantee that an agreement could be reached. And if an agreement were reached, it would certainly be short of what the United States might want. But the test of a U.S.-Iran negotiation is not how it measures up against an ideal arrangement but how it measures up against the alternatives of bombing or doing nothing.

U.S. prewar intelligence on Iraq was horrifically wrong on the key question of Iraq's possession of WMDs, and President Bush ignored the intelligence to assert falsely a connection between Saddam Hussein and September 11. This alone is sufficient reason to be skeptical of the Bush administration's statements on Iran.

On December 3, 2007, the U.S. intelligence community undercut President Bush's case against Iran and shredded the president's already diminished credibility. As required by Congress, the National Intelligence Council published an unclassified version of its just completed National Intelligence Estimate (NIE) assessment of Iran's nuclear program. In its main conclusion, all sixteen U.S. intelligence agencies assessed, "We judge with high confidence that in fall 2003, Tehran halted its nuclear weapons program." This conclusion eliminated any basis for a U.S. attack on Iran, and even several leading neoconservatives unhappily conceded in print that war was off the table and the United States might have to consider negotiation.

On October 17, 2007, six weeks before the NIE was made public, President Bush held a press conference at the White House. Russian president Vladimir Putin was in Iran on a state visit and had said he saw "no evidence to suggest Iran wants to build a nuclear bomb." Bush was asked about this:

REPORTER: But you definitely believe Iran wants to build a nuclear weapon?

PRESIDENT BUSH: I think so long—until they suspend and/or make it clear that they—that their statements aren't real, yeah, I believe they want to have the capacity, the knowledge, in order to make a nuclear weapon. And I know it's in the world's interest to prevent them from doing so. I believe that the Iranian— if Iran had a nuclear weapon, it would be a dangerous threat to world peace. But this—we got a leader in Iran who has announced that he wants to destroy Israel. So I've told people that if you're interested in avoiding World War III, it seems like you ought to be interested in preventing them from have [sic] the knowledge necessary to make a nuclear weapon.

The CIA had already briefed Bush on the substance of the NIE without any apparent effect. The episode provided another example of the irrelevance of strategy to President Bush's conduct of national security. Even if Bush believed, in his now-famous gut, that the NIE's conclusions were wrong, he could only damage his goal of building international and domestic support for action against Iran with extreme statements that he knew would soon be contradicted by his own intelligence agencies. Yet this is precisely what Bush did. Ironically, the NIE's conclusion that Iran did not have a nuclear weapons program did not change the undisputed fact that it has a uranium enrichment program that allows it to produce the fissile material for a nuclear weapon, which is the most difficult hurdle in the atom bomb making process. Bush's reckless rhetoric severely undercut his ability to garner support to deal with this still real problem.

The NIE concluded that Iran halted its nuclear weapons program in 2003 because it feared international isolation. Moreover, "Tehran's decision to halt its nuclear weapons program suggests it is less determined to develop nuclear weapons than we have been judging since 2005. Our assessment that the program probably was halted primarily in response to international pressure suggests Iran may be more vulnerable to influence on the issue than we judged previously."

This punctured the image of Iran as a country of mad mullahs bent on acquiring nuclear weapons that they might use in a suicidal mission against the United States or Israel. Implicit in this analysis of Iran's behavior is that Iran is a rational actor open to a deal that enhances its security and acknowledges its role as an important regional power.

Some of the administration's other charges against Iran defy common sense. In his Reno speech, President Bush accused

Iran of arming the Taliban in Afghanistan while his administration has, at various times, accused Iran of giving weapons to both Sunni and Shiite insurgents in Iraq. The Taliban are Salafi jihadis, Sunni fundamentalists who consider Shiites apostates deserving of death. In power, the Taliban brutally repressed Afghanistan's Shiites and nearly provoked a war with Iran when they murdered Iranian diplomats inside the Iranian consulate in the northern city of Mazar-i-Sharif. Iraq's Sunni insurgents are either Salafi jihadis or Baathists, the political party that started the Iran-Iraq War.

The Iranian regime may believe it has a strategic interest in keeping U.S. forces tied down in the Iraqi quagmire since this, in the Iranian view, makes an attack on Iran unlikely. U.S. clashes with the Mahdi Army complicate the American military effort in Iraq, and it is plausible that Iran might provide some weapons—including armor-penetrating IEDs—to the Mahdi Army and its splinter factions. Overall, however, Iran has no interest in the success of the Mahdi Army. Moqtada al-Sadr has made Iraqi nationalism his political platform. He has attacked the SIIC for its pro-Iranian leanings and challenged Iraq's most important religious figure, Ayatollah Sistani, himself an Iranian citizen. Asked about charges that Iran was organizing Iraqi insurgents, Iran's deputy foreign minister, Abbas Araghchi, told the *Financial Times* on May 10, 2007, "The whole idea is unreasonable. Why should we do that? Why should we undermine a government in Iraq that we support more than anybody else?"

The United States cannot now undo President Bush's strategic gift to Iran. But importantly, the most pro-Iranian Shiite political party is the one least hostile to the United States. In the battle now under way between the SIIC and Moqtada al-Sadr for control of southern Iraq and of the central government in

Baghdad, the United States and Iran are on the same side. The U.S. has good reason to worry about Iran's activities in Iraq. But contrary to the Bush administration's allegations—allegations reiterated by both General David Petraeus and Ambassador Ryan Crocker in their congressional testimony in the fall of 2007—Iran does not oppose Iraq's new political order. In fact, Iran is the major beneficiary of the American-induced changes in Iraq since 2003.

4

Turkey

In the summer of 2007, the Pew Charitable Trust conducted a poll in Turkey. Nine percent of Turks had a favorable opinion of the United States while 83 percent viewed the U.S. unfavorably. Turkish newspapers announced the news with headlines boasting "Turkey most anti-American country in the world."

The Bush administration has cited Turkey as a model for the Islamic world—secular, democratic, and a close American ally. (Turkey is the second most populous NATO ally after Germany.) It is never good news when the country you cite as your model hates you.

Being unpopular has consequences. On October 17, 2007, the Turkish parliament authorized its military to cross into northern Iraq, ostensibly in pursuit of the PKK, a Turkish Kurdish rebel group that has used bases in the no-man's-land just inside Iraq's mountainous borders with Turkey and Iran to stage terrorist attacks inside Turkey. Subsequently, Turkey began air strikes into northern Iraq and in February 2008 sent ten thousand soldiers across the border.

Turkey threatened to destabilize the one secure, democratic, and pro-American part of Iraq, the Kurdistan region. With 160,000 U.S. troops more than fully occupied in Baghdad and central Iraq, Turkey's actions were not those of a close ally. They were a poke in the eye of President Bush, who had made Iraq the signature project of his eight years in office.

In 2000—the last year of Bill Clinton's presidency—the same Pew poll showed that 60 percent of Turks viewed the United States favorably. In the 1990s, Turks were exceptionally concerned about the fate of two European Muslim peoples—the Bosnians and the Kosovar Albanians—who had once been part of the Ottoman Empire. Balkan Muslims had long constituted the elite of the Ottoman Empire and, as it fell apart in the nineteenth century, hundreds of thousands moved to Turkey. In 1993, Turkish president Turgut Ozal told me that his country had two million Muslims of Bosnian origin (the same number as in Bosnia), which was why war in Bosnia had become the top issue in his country. In 1995, President Clinton took military and diplomatic action to end the Bosnia war and in 1999 launched an eighty-four-day air war that drove the Serb army out of Kosovo. Turks were impressed that the United States acted against a Christian nation (Serbia) to save two Muslim peoples from genocide and aggression. They were also impressed by the competence of the American operation: not only did the United States handily defeat the Serb Army but it did so without the loss of a single NATO soldier in hostile action in either the Bosnia or Kosovo wars, or during the many years of NATO peace enforcement that followed.

In 2001, George W. Bush benefited from his predecessors'

high standing in Turkey. After the September 11 attacks, Turkey was one of the first countries to side with America militarily, authorizing its forces to fight alongside the United States in Afghanistan on November 1, 2001—weeks before the Taliban regime fell and other American allies clamored to join what looked like an easy peace to police. Later, Turkey made a significant troop contribution to the post-Taliban, NATO-led stabilization force in Afghanistan.

Turks, however, overwhelmingly opposed the Iraq War. Living next to Iraq, they did not see the threat that the Bush administration hyped to the American people but did foresee the chaos that the war would likely produce. Other U.S. allies that opposed the war had the possibility of sitting on the sidelines. Turkey, however, was critical to the Pentagon's war plans, which involved having the 4th Infantry Division cross Turkey to open a second front in Kurdish northern Iraq.

The Bush administration's diplomatic efforts to persuade Turkey to participate in the war effort were ineffective and inept. At the request of Deputy Defense Secretary Paul Wolfowitz, I participated in Pentagon briefings for Turkish leader Recep Tayyip Erdogan in November 2002, and I could see that he and his team were underwhelmed by the "evidence" the neoconservatives presented about the Iraqi threat. In the end, Erdogan felt he had no choice but to go along. However he and the Turkish General Staff demanded a steep price. In addition to billions of dollars in aid, Turkey insisted on sending its own troops into Kurdish-controlled Iraqi territory. Although the Iraqi Kurds warned that they would fight any Turkish troops that did enter their territory, the Bush administration gave in to the Turkish demands.

Even so, Turkish public opinion opposed cooperation with

the U.S. war effort and proud Turks denounced the billions in promised aid as a bribe, which it was. On March 1, 2003, the Turkish parliament voted affirmatively on the U.S. request for transit rights for the 4th Infantry Division but by a margin that fell four votes short of the required absolute majority. To this day, it is not clear whether the Erdogan government engineered the narrow defeat or was caught by surprise by an assertive parliament representing its constituents. The strongest opposition came not from Erdogan's party, which mostly supported the U.S. request, but from the opposition CHP, the party most closely aligned with the supposedly pro-U.S. Turkish military. Although the vote actually spared the United States the folly of a decision that would have begun the Iraq War with fighting between America's Turkish and Kurdish allies, the neoconservatives were furious. They vented their outrage (off the record, of course) to favored journalists, warning that Turkey would pay a price. Later, as fingers started to be pointed at Rumsfeld, Wolfowitz, and Feith for the planning failures that allowed Baghdad to descend into chaos in the weeks that followed the U.S. takeover, Bush administration officials came up with a highly creative excuse: it was all Turkey's fault. If Turkey had only allowed the 4th Infantry Division to cross its territory, enough troops would have arrived in Baghdad to prevent the widespread looting. This explanation ignores the inconvenient detail that the Bush administration never even thought about providing public security or protecting Iraqi public institutions, but infuriated the Turks who now found themselves blamed for the Bush administration's incompetence. Turkish views of the United States declined further when the ineptness of the American occupation became apparent and the supposed WMD were never found.

American analysts, both inside the government and out, have tended to reduce Turkey's concerns about the Iraq War to one issue: the Kurds. According to this view, Turkey was and is afraid that the U.S. intervention in Iraq will lead to the breakup of the country and the emergence of an independent Kurdistan with irredentist ambitions that would include Turkey's Kurdish southeast. Turkey is, of course, concerned about the Kurdish question in both Iraq and Turkey, but it has a much more nuanced and sophisticated understanding of the issue than most Washington analysts. Furthermore, its views on Iraq, and the disaster caused by the American intervention, are not nearly as one-dimensional as most American analysts seem to believe.

While Americans often see the Kurdish question as a seamless whole, Turkey has consistently looked at six million Kurds in northern Iraq very differently from how it sees the aspirations of the eighteen million Kurds who live in Turkey itself. In fact, Turkey, more than any other country, made possible the emergence of an independent Kurdistan in the territory of Iraq. And, unlike what Bush has done, this was no accident.

Turkey's relations with the Iraqi Kurds go back to the final days of the Persian Gulf War. While the first Bush administration had a policy of no contact with the Iraqi Kurdish leaders (for fear of offending Turkey), Turkish president Turgut Ozal secretly opened contacts with PUK leader Jalal Talabani, inviting him to Ankara in March 1991. Later that month, the Iraqi Kurds rose up against Saddam and, by the end of the month, Iraqi Army counterattacks had driven two million Kurds to seek safety on the mountainsides that were Kurdistan's borders with Turkey and Iran. In spite of having called for Iraqis to overthrow Saddam, President George H. W. Bush assumed no responsibility for the humanitarian disaster unfolding on the Turkish and Iranian borders and being broadcast around the world by CNN. It was Turkish president Ozal who demanded action and ultimately pushed the reluctant Americans to create a safe haven for the Kurds in northern Iraq. Even as this safe haven took on the characteristics of a sovereign state—electing a parliament, forming a government, and organizing a military—Turkey provided Iraqi Kurdistan its main commercial access to the outside world, encouraged Turkish business to be present there, and, most important, allowed the United States and Britain to use the air base at Incirlik to fly patrols that protected Kurdistan from Saddam's army. After Saddam's fall, Turkey aggressively promoted Turkish investment in Iraqi Kurdistan (as of 2007, some 80 to 90 percent of foreign investment in Kurdistan came from Turkey).

Turkey's relationship with Iraqi Kurdistan is, of course, complicated by the fact that Turkey is home to half the world's Kurds. Fourteen to eighteen million Kurds live in Turkey, far more than the six million in Iraq or the eight million to ten million in Iran. Most live in the Turkey's impoverished southeast but millions have migrated to Turkey's more prosperous west. Istanbul is the world's most populous Kurdish city.

For decades, Turkey's nationalist leaders denied there were any Kurds in the country at all. Speaking Kurdish was illegal; any display of Kurdish nationalism was punishable by long prison sentences; and the nationalists insisted the inhabitants of the southeast were "Mountain Turks" who had, regrettably forgotten their mother tongue. Turkey's military, with its self-awarded mission of guardian of the nation, was and still is vehemently anti-Kurdish.

Turkey's harsh repression of any expression of a Kurdish identity—combined with the grueling poverty of the southeast—eventually provoked a violent Kurdish reaction. On November 28, 1978, Abdullah Ocalan, a university dropout with an uncanny physical and psychological resemblance to Stalin, founded the PKK, a political party with the goal of creating an independent Marxist Kurdish state carved out of what is now southeast Turkey. In 1984, the PKK—the initials are taken from Kurdish for the Kurdistan Workers' Party— began an armed struggle for independence. The war lasted fifteen years and cost at least thirty thousand lives, most of them PKK fighters and Kurdish civilians. The PKK's often brutal tactics earned it a place on the State Department's list of terrorist organizations. It assassinated Kurdish village guards (Kurds enrolled, not always voluntarily, in a progovernment militia) along with Kurdish teachers and civil servants who were targeted as representatives of the Turkish state. It was as brutal toward its own cadres. Recruits spent long hours studying the jargon-laced speeches of its leader Ocalan and had to abide by a strict disciplinary code that prohibited marriage and sexual relations. Infractions were punishable by death, as was dissent and trying to quit the PKK.*

In response, the Turkish military imposed martial law in the southeast, blanketing the area with troops, mainly conscripts, to lock down vast swaths of territory. Taking a page from Saddam Hussein's book, the army destroyed hundreds of Kurdish villages, wrecking the rural economy. Displaced villagers swelled southeast Turkey's cities, which were largely unable to house,

---

* For the account of Ocalan's career and downfall in this paragraph and the paragraphs that follow, I make use of the extraordinary reporting done by Aliza Marcus in *Blood and Belief: The PKK and the Kurdish Fight for Independence,* NYU Press, 2007.

school, or employ the new arrivals. As brutal as they were, Turkey's tactics deprived the PKK—a guerrilla movement living off
the land—of the supplies it needed to function.

While Abdullah Ocalan made the PKK into a political and
military powerhouse, he also helped destroy it. Ocalan had one
overriding interest: himself. From his villa in Damascus, he
gave orders to his field commanders that bore only a limited
relationship to the reality on the ground, about which Ocalan
was remarkably uninterested. Commanders who followed his
orders unnecessarily lost fighters; those who didn't risked Ocalan's wrath, which could be fatal. Above all, Ocalan wanted to
remain in charge of the PKK. Like Stalin, Ocalan purged and
murdered many of his most successful associates. He was luke-
warm toward Kurdish political parties trying to operate legally
in Turkey (such parties were routinely closed down by the Turkish government and then reestablished under a new name) and
blocked a general uprising at a time when it might have been
opportune. He was afraid of any development in Kurdish politics that he did not completely control.

Syria supported the PKK because it saw the organization
as a useful tool in its ongoing disputes with its large neighbor.
Syrian-Turkish relations have been sour since the 1930s, when
Atatürk seized Antioch from Syria and annexed it to Turkey. Syrian maps still show the province as part of Syria. In the 1980s,
and 1990s, the two countries feuded over Turkey's massive dam
projects on the Euphrates, which threatened to deprive down-
stream Syria and Iraq of vital waters. The 1991 collapse of the
Soviet Union, Syria's close ally and main provider of military
equipment, left Damascus isolated and exposed. Turkey, which
had been on the winning side of the Cold War, warned it would

attack militarily unless Damascus ended its support for the PKK. Ocalan suddenly became a major liability and the Syrians gave him a choice: be extradited to Turkey or leave. Unfortunately for him, he had no place to go. Russia and Greece refused to take him, and he ended up in Italy and then Nairobi, where the Greek ambassador put him up at his residence.

Turkish intelligence tracked him down through his cell phone. The Greek ambassador told him he could not stay and on the morning of February 16, a Kenyan escort arrived at the ambassador's residence to take Ocalan to a plane bound for the Netherlands, or so Ocalan thought. In fact, the Kenyans delivered him to a jet chartered by Turkish special forces, who flew him straight to Turkey.

Once he realized what had happened, Ocalan did everything possible to save his life. On the plane, he told his captors: "I love my country. My mother is a Turk. If I can be of service, I will." The Turks videotaped the craven scene and released the video. In the days following his capture, mobs of angry Kurds attacked Greek diplomatic missions in Europe, blaming Greece for having betrayed their leader. Turkey's leaders could not have dreamed of a better outcome. They had captured public enemy number one and Kurds retaliated against Greece.

At his trial, Ocalan expressed sorrow for the Turkish soldiers killed by the PKK but never mentioned the thousands of Kurdish lives lost in the struggle. He praised Ataturk, the founder of the Turkish republic, who denied the existence of a separate Kurdish identity. He denounced the armed struggle and, in August 1999, Ocalan ordered the PKK to stand down the insurgency and implement a cease-fire, which it did. At this point Turkey had won the war against the PKK. Instead of consolidating the victory by being magnanimous, Turkey took a hard line line toward rank-and-file PKK cadres and in so doing gave the organization a second chance.

Turgut Ozal, the president who opened a dialogue with the Iraqi Kurds, also had an enlightened attitude toward Turkey's Kurds. After replacing President Kenan Evren, the ironfisted general who had seized power in a 1980 coup, Ozal in 1990 ended the ban on the Kurdish language and, in a truly radical step, referred to the mountain Turks as "Kurds." Ozal's death in 1993 from a heart attack was mourned both in northern Iraq and southeast Turkey, but his successors continued his policies. As a condition of starting talks to join the European Union, the EU countries demanded that Turkey bring its human rights practices in line with European standards. Rather than suppressing or assimilating national minorities, the EU emphasizes recognizing each distinctive community. Turkey was required to offer schooling and broadcasting in Kurdish, to end its ban on parents giving their children Kurdish names, and to end the prosecution for peaceably advocating Kurdish political rights. As important, Turkey ended martial law in the southeast, paving the way for local elections that put Kurds in charge of the municipalities in the southeast, including Diyarbakir. While these local mayors are sometimes harassed by the national authorities (scores of cases have been filed against Osman Baydemir, the Diyarbakir mayor), they have empowered Turkey's Kurds and channeled Kurdish politics away from nationalism and into practicalities of local government.

Political reform in Turkey, combined with the PKK's military defeat, has transformed the Kurdish movement in Turkey from being separatist to being primarily focused on civil rights. Many Turkish Kurds now recognize they are far better off as part of an increasingly prosperous Turkey, which may eventually join the European Union, than having their own impoverished and landlocked state in Turkey's southeast. The PKK-allied parties have become fervent supporters of Turkish membership in the EU, even organizing seminars examining that goal at the European parliament in Brussels.

As Turkey's border with Iraq moves east from the trijunction with Syria at the confluence of the Tigris and Habur rivers, it quickly becomes nearly impenetrable high mountain terrain. In the 1980s, the Iraqi side of the border was the last redoubt of the KDP guerillas fighting Saddam's regime. After Saddam crushed the KDP in 1988, the PKK moved in, sharing the area with smugglers and criminals. In 1991, Iraqi authority disappeared completely from the Kurdistan region and the weak Kurdish authorities were, by themselves, in no position to challenge the PKK in what had for decades been a mountainous no-man's-land. The PKK used these mountains as a base for attacks into Turkey, although most of the PKK operations—then and now—originated from within Turkey. Both the KDP and the PUK saw the PKK as a potential threat to their preeminence in Iraqi Kurdistan and both parties disagreed with its use of terrorism as a tactic, fearing terrorism could tar Kurds with the same brush that so damaged the Palestine Liberation Organization prior to the Oslo peace accords. The KDP also depended on Turkey for trade and its access to the outside world. In the mid-1990s, KDP peshmerga fought alongside Turkish troops inside Iraqi Kurdistan against the PKK. After Ocalan's capture and the PKK's unilateral declaration of a cease-fire, neither Turkey nor the Kurdistan authorities concerned themselves with the PKK fighters who took over the base of the Kurdistan Democratic Party of Iran (KDP-I,

an anti-Tehran Kurdish group that operated out of Iraqi territory) on Qandil Mountain on the Iraqi side of the Iraq-Iran
border.

With Ocalan's capture and the cease-fire, the PKK fighters
entered a limbo that risked evolving into oblivion. Leaving their
mountain redoubts in Turkey or bases in northern Iraq meant
arrest and a prolonged prison term. Remaining in their bases
meant irrelevance combined with privation, boredom, and
harsh winter weather. The PKK, which had begun its armed
struggle for independence and socialism, now asked only for
amnesty so that the ordinary fighters could return home (the
leaders largely understood that they were not going to be am-
nestied). The Turkish military saw no need to offer amnesty to
terrorists whom it thought it had vanquished.

With Turkey unwilling to budge on their now minimal demands, the PKK eventually calculated that resumed operations
was the only way they could attract attention to their cause,
and more importantly to themselves. In 2007, the particular
combination of tense relations between Turkey's Islamic AK
Party government and the devoutly secular military, elections
for president and parliament, and a failing U.S. mission in Iraq
gave the renewed PKK operations an impact that must have
exceeded its leaders' wildest dreams.

The generals who designed Turkey's constitution and electoral system after the 1980 military coup had three goals in
mind: first, to ensure a major role in the government for the
"Deep State," an informal grouping that includes the Turkish
General Staff, the intelligence services, and some senior diplomats; second, to preserve the secular character of the Turkish republic; and third to suppress Kurdish nationalism. With
a proportional representation system requiring a 10 percent

threshold for entry into the parliament, Turkey's electoral system was designed to produce weak coalitions among Turkey's multiple and indistinguishable secular parties while, because of the threshold, keeping the Kurdish nationalist parties out of the parliament. In 2002, the system proved, from the perspective of the Deep State, too clever by half. While collectively winning 60 percent of the vote, Turkey's secular parties had become so fractured that only one, the CHP (Atatürk's Republican Party), made it across the threshold, garnering 17 percent of the vote. Meanwhile, a moderate Islamic Party, the AK, won 34 percent of the vote, partly because Turkish voters were fed up with their feuding—and nonperforming—secular politicians. Thanks to the electoral system, the AK's 34 percent of the vote translated into a two-thirds majority in the parliament. And with that majority the AK was able to put together a strong government that produced results and became popular. The Deep State, and in particular the General Staff, considered the AK a threat to secularism even though, aside from a quickly aborted proposal to criminalize adultery, the AK never promoted an Islamic agenda in government. But, as important, the Deep State resented the AK as a politically powerful force that was beyond its control. Through its entire tenure in government, the military worked to undermine the AK. The vote to deny the United States military transit rights in 2003 was one such occasion (Erdogan had promised Bush that the 4th Infantry Division could cross Turkey to northern Iraq, while the military worked with the CHP to block parliamentary approval). When the PKK resumed military operations, the Deep State seized on this as a club to use on the AK.

In 2007, Turkey's parliament was to elect a new president in May and parliamentary elections were due in the fall. Erdogan's choice for president was Abdullah Gül, his foreign minister and close friend. The Deep State opposed Gül, ostensibly because it would insult Atatürk's legacy to have a woman wearing a headscarf (as does Gül's wife) in the presidential palace. While the president's powers are limited in Turkey, he does serve as a check on the prime minister and government, and the last thing the military wanted was for the AK to control both offices. When the Deep State blocked Gül's election—via a dubious Supreme Court ruling—Erdogan advanced parliamentary elections to July and won a decisive victory. The new parliament then elected Gül as president, but the military simmered with anger over its defeat. The PKK issue proved a convenient vehicle to challenge the government's patriotism. Unless the AK authorized military strikes against PKK bases in northern Iraq, the military threatened to portray it as disloyal, which in turn might provide—as it had in the past—the pretext for a coup.

Objectively, the PKK is not much of a threat. Militarily, it is a pale shadow of the organization that waged a fifteen-year war in the 1980s and 1990s. Politically, as noted, its agenda is amnesty, not independence. It has committed atrocities. On October 21, 2007, the PKK attacked a Turkish garrison, killing seventeen Turkish soldiers and capturing eight who were taken from Turkey to a PKK base in northern Iraq. (The Kurdistan Regional Government intervened to secure the release of the eight, who were then prosecuted in Turkey for having been captured). The PKK has also engaged in bombings of civilian targets, although it is almost certainly not responsible for all the terrorist acts for which it is accused. In fact, some of these may be carried out by the Deep State itself. In one notorious case, a crowd caught a supposed PKK bomber just after a deadly attack in Semdinli, in southeast Turkey. The terrorist turned out to be a Turkish intelligence operative whose mission was later praised by the head of Turkish General Staff.

Politically, however, the PKK emerged in 2007 as the proxy issue in a battle between the AK and the Deep State being fought over secularism and power. When the military insisted on going into northern Iraq to attack the PKK, the AK felt it had no choice but to go along. However, both Gül and Erdogan sought to limit the scope of the hostilities and to avoid a direct confrontation with the Iraqi Kurds.

Nonetheless, Turkey's military intervention—first in the form of air strikes in late 2007 and then sending ten thousand soldiers across in February 2008—risked a dramatic escalation of the Iraq War. Kurdistan's President Massoud Barzani warned that intervention was a game that two could play, implicitly threatening to incite an uprising by Kurds in southeast Turkey. Turkey's military then threatened to target Barzani personally.

The Bush administration, which had largely ignored Turkey's concerns over the PKK for four years, responded with solicitous assurances to the Turkish government about future steps against the PKK and veiled warnings against military action. But, as the crisis built up in September 2007, President Bush quietly let lapse the appointment of retired Air Force general Joseph Ralston, who had been named the year before as the president's special envoy for countering PKK terrorism. As a former NATO commander, Ralston could speak credibly to the Turkish General Staff, whom he knew well. However, Ralston was given a very limited mandate, had little support, and was only part-time. The collapse of his mission only served to reinforce the Turkish belief that their concerns were not being taken seriously. Many Turks believe that the U.S. unwillingness to go after the PKK, an organization the United States deems to be terrorist, is intended to punish Turkey for the 2003 vote.

The next administration will have a big task in repairing relations with Turkey. Simply having a new president will help, given how little Turks think of George W. Bush. But, the new U.S. administration will have to address two issues that are at the root of Turkish dissatisfaction and are, in the Turks' view, the consequences of the U.S. takeover of Iraq: the resurgent PKK and the prospective Kurdish annexation of the oil-rich city and province of Kirkuk. In both cases, the substance of the issue may be less important than rectifying a Turkish perception that the United States is indifferent to their concerns.

Turkey's 2008 invasion of Iraqi Kurdistan's border areas was a military disaster, although one significantly covered up by the Turkish General Staff. Scores of Turkish soldiers died—not at the hands of the PKK, which is, as noted, a largely ineffectual organizaton—but from exposure. Although the operation was undertaken in winter, Turkish troops were not adequately equipped for the harsh weather in Kurdistan's mountains, and many died when rapidly shifting weather prevented helicopters from picking them up as planned. But, more importantly, there is no military solution to the PKK problem. Having been up to Qandil Mountain (back in 1992, when the Iranian KDP was there), I could see why this terrain is so good for guerrillas. There are caves to shelter from aerial bombardment and any land assault is necessarily telegraphed long in advance, giving the guerrillas plenty of time to disperse. Turkey has defined victory against the PKK as killing all its cadres, and this it cannot achieve. The PKK cannot do serious harm to Turkey but it can launch the occasional attack or act of terrorism.

While doing little actual harm to the PKK militarily, Turkey has given it an enormous boost politically and psychologically. Before 2007, the PKK was largely forgotten elsewhere in the world; it was just another defeated and discredited guerrilla movement. Turkey's *response* to PKK attacks has put the group on the front pages and near the top of the agenda in European capitals as well as Washington. And, if as a result of PKK outrages, Turkey ends up attacking Iraqi Kurdistan, so much the better for the PKK. The KRG is led by parties that are the PKK's rivals. Thus the PKK has every incentive to launch new attacks and the more spectacular the better.

The United States should have two goals: to prevent the PKK from launching attacks and to contain the fallout from any attack so that it does not have the consequences desired by the PKK. The United States is not much more capable militarily than Turkey in defeating the PKK, and U.S. generals, understandably, have no interest in expanding the American military mission in Iraq to fight an organization that has never targeted the U.S. The United States could help by encouraging Turkey—quietly and behind the scenes—to take the minimal steps that likely would make the PKK go away. Turkey will not negotiate with an organization that it sees as a terrorist organization (and which has committed hundreds of terrorist acts) but, in this case, negotiations are probably not necessary. An unconditional amnesty for most fighters, combined with some employment opportunities, would likely be sufficient to get them off the mountains. Amnesty is not, as many Turks see it, an admission of weakness or an absolution for PKK crimes. It is simply the practical recognition that, if the PKK guerrillas cannot go home, their only other choice is to remain in the mountains as fighters.

Of course, Turkey also needs to address the social and

political grievances that enabled the PKK to win so much support among Turkey's Kurds. These include continuing the reforms now under way but also giving Kurds a much easier way to participate—as Kurds—in Turkey's national life. Right now, Turkey bans ethnic parties from competing in elections, and has successfully closed Kurdish parties operating under politically neutral names. (Once banned, these parties are established again under a new name. Given the slow pace of the Turkish judiciary, a newly formed party can expect a two-to three-year run before it is again banned.) Even if Turkey keeps the prohibition on explicitly ethnic parties, it ought not to ban parties because their membership is heavily Kurdish and their program is to promote Kurdish rights.

While the United States understandably is reluctant to fight the PKK, it can encourage the Kurdistan Regional Government (KRG) to do more to prevent Kurdish territory from being used as a base for attacks into Turkey. The KRG peshmerga are even less capable than the Americans and the Turks in launching an assault on the PKK positions, but, more importantly, there is no stomach within the KRG or the Kurdistan public to fight fellow Kurds. After escalating Turkish threats in 2007, the KRG established checkpoints on the roads that lead to the PKK camps and began more actively to interdict supplies and people. Prime Minister Nechirvan Barzani warned the local Kurdish media against praising the PKK and sought to soften the rhetoric between the KRG and Turkey. These steps were useful but should have come sooner.

Prior to the 2003 war, and in its immediate aftermath, Turkey proclaimed itself to be the protector of Iraq's Turkmen population. Turkmen are ethnic Turks who were left behind as the Ottoman Empire collapsed. Many of these Turkmen live in Kirkuk, a city and surrounding province of the same name that borders Iraqi Kurdistan. Kurds claim Kirkuk as a historic part of Kurdistan, and the 1992 draft Kurdistan constitution made Kirkuk the region's capital, even though Saddam Hussein controlled the city. Kirkuk also happens to be atop one of Iraq's largest oil fields. Turks suspect that the Kurds want Kirkuk because its oil would give them the economic wherewithal for full independence while the Kurds believe Turkey has manufactured the Turkmen issue to keep Kirkuk out of their hands. (And, not without reason. Until the late 1990s, Turkish governments almost never referred to Iraqi Turkmens. Turkey then claimed Iraq had three million Turkmens, or a population about half that of the Kurds. In the December 2005 elections, however, the Iraqi Turkmen parties won just one seat in the Council of Representatives. Since voting in that election was almost entirely along ethnic and religious lines, this would indicate a Sunni Turkmen population of about 150,000. Shiite Turkmen, thought to equal in number the Sunni Turkmen, voted in significant numbers for the Shiite religious parties, so the total Turkmen population—Sunni and Shiite—might be double this amount.)

Article 140 of Iraq's constitution says that Kirkuk's status will be settled by a referendum. (It should have been held before the end of 2007 but was postponed.) Based on the 2005 voting, it appears all but certain that the Kurds will win the referendum. While Turkey no longer threatens military action to stop Kurdistan's annexation of Kirkuk, it nonetheless strongly opposes that result. Inevitably, a Kirkuk plebiscite will leave the losers—likely the Turkmens and Arabs—frustrated and angry. Because of its close relationship with the Kurds, the United States can do a lot diplomatically to promote solutions in

Kirkuk that will make inclusion in Kurdistan more palatable to the losers. These measures could include an outsized role for the minority communities in governing Kirkuk, special representation in the Kurdistan government and parliament, and local autonomy for the ethnic communities, to include having their own schools and police forces. Prime Minister Barzani has endorsed most of these ideas, and the U.S. could help make them happen. However, in spite of the widespread recognition that Kirkuk could be a powderkeg both inside Iraq and by bringing in Turkey, U.S. diplomacy has been largely absent in terms of finding solutions.

Turkey seems to accept the reality of an independent Kurdistan, even if it wishes it hadn't happened. General Kenan Evren, the military dictator who made himself president in the 1980s, has a reputation for being anti-Kurdish, going back to the harsh measures he imposed in southeast Turkey during the early phases of the war against the PKK. In 2007, he told *Sabah* newspaper that "A Kurdish state was founded" in Iraq and that Turkey must get used to it. He went on to observe that the situation of the Kurds in Turkey was quite different from Iraq, and it does not follow that a Kurdish state in Iraq means one will be carved out of Turkey.

Some Turks go further and argue that an independent Kurdistan on the territory of the former Iraq is an advantage to Turkey. They point out that the Kurds are secular, pro-Western, aspire to be democratic, and are not Arabs. In short, their place in the Middle East is a lot like that of the Turks themselves. Furthermore, an independent pro-Western Kurdistan would be a buffer to an Iranian-dominated Shiite Arab Iraq. These analysts also note that landlocked Kurdistan is dependent on someone and that should be Turkey.

Kurdistan's leaders also recognize the importance of Turkey. Both Nechirvan Barzani, the prime minister of Iraqi Kurdistan, and Barham Salih, the Kurd who is deputy prime minister of Iraq, have worked hard to link Kurdistan to Turkey economically and politically. The KRG has given Turkish companies multibillion-dollar public service contracts to build the region's two international airports, roads, and two new university campuses. The KRG has also encouraged Turkish companies to apply for oil exploration contracts awarded by the Kurdistan government and not Baghdad.

The stakes in Turkey are high. The AK government wants to move Turkey from the outmoded semiauthoritarian system set up by Atatürk into being a full-fledged democracy closely linked to, and eventually part of, the European Union. Naturally, this is resisted by the beneficiaries of the old system, notably the top ranks of the Turkish military. The Bush administration's careless handling of relations with Turkey has turned an ally into a country whose people are among the most anti-American in the world. As the AK looks west, its rivals may find it politically popular to take Turkey in the opposite direction, including building much closer ties with anti-American forces in the region, including Iran and Syria. Turkey's internal power struggle could play out in an unwelcome way in Iraq and the Middle East while undermining the Islamic Middle East's one stable democracy.

Several of the prominent neoconservative architects of the Iraq War had close ties to Turkey. They hoped for an Iraq that would be a reliable U.S. ally like Turkey. They may have ended up with a Turkey more like Iraq.

5

Cleaning Up the Mess

As we have seen, the Iraq War's unintended consequences include an empowered Iran, civil war in a disintegrated Iraq, and an alienated Turkey. Elsewhere in the Middle East, Syria is more confident, Israel less secure, and peace between Israel and Palestinians more remote. The United States' traditional Sunni Arab allies regard what America has done in Iraq with horror (for the attack on an Arab nation, for the incompetence of the occupation, and for turning a Sunni Arab bulwark over to the Shiites and Iran) and their peoples are now rabidly anti-American. Around the world, respect for the United States is at an all-time low.

What has been so casually wrought is not readily reversed. And the United States cannot begin to recover from the Iraq fiasco until it figures a way out of Iraq. Unfortunately, it was a lot easier to get in than to get out.

There is no shortage of ideas as to what should be done

in Iraq. Hardly a week goes by (or so it seems) without some scholar or politician contributing an op-ed to a major newspaper with an idea for dealing with one aspect or another of the Iraq imbroglio. These plans mostly consist of things Iraqis need to do. But it is not as if ideas are put forward that no Iraqi ever thought of. If the Iraqis were willing and able to agree on a program of national reconciliation, revenue sharing, or constitutional amendments, they would have. The divisions in Iraq run deep, which is why Iraqis cannot agree among themselves. The United States needs an Iraq strategy that does not depend on the Iraqis; it needs one that it can implement itself.

Three principles should drive a future U.S. strategy for Iraq. First, it should promote U.S. interests, which may not be the same as those of Iraq's multiple factions. Second, it should be realistic, which is to say it should relate to Iraqi realities. And, third, it should be feasible, meaning a course of action that can actually be implemented.

Iraq does not—and never did—pose a serious threat to U.S. national security. An unstable Pakistan, a nuclear-armed North Korea, an Iran pursuing nuclear capabilities, and al-Qaeda are all far more dangerous. Iraq diverted President Bush from these other threats and as a result they became more dangerous. In order to mobilize resources—including the now-overstretched armed forces—to face real threats to American security, the United States must get out of Iraq.

Nonetheless, the manner of the exit matters. Al-Qaeda was not in Iraq before Bush invaded but it is there now. The United States has a strong interest in the Sunni Awakening continuing to oppose al-Qaeda and remaining stronger than al-Qaeda. We do not wish to be seen as having been driven out or as irresponsibly indifferent to the fate of those we left behind, and we do not want our troops fighting their way out. It would therefore be advantageous if we could leave Iraq more stable than it is now. Finally, we have a moral and pragmatic obligation to those who took our side in the Iraq War. This includes the Kurds, who were our military allies in 2003 (taking more casualties in the battle to overthrow Saddam than any other ally), as well the thousands of Iraqis who have supported U.S. troops and diplomats as interpreters and in many other jobs.

The Iraq War's boosters insist there is more to be done. Senator John McCain says that U.S. troops must remain in Iraq until it becomes "a democratic ally." He also says that Iraq must not become "a pawn of Iran." President Bush, however, has given up on both goals. He supports the Shiite theocrats that govern southern Iraq and dominate the federal govenment. In central Iraq, he supports the Baathists who lead the Sunni Awakening. He has no intention of foisting Iraq's constitutionally guaranteed freedoms or rule of law on either group. Equally, Bush is making no effort to counter Iran's substantial influence in Iraq. On the contrary, Bush embraces an Iraqi government led by a prime minister and political parties closely associated with Iran. In 2008, Bush had U.S. troops fight on behalf of the pro-Iranian Shiite establishment against Moqtada al-Sadr's more nationalist movement. President Bush knows that promoting democracy or opposing Iran in Iraq would require more U.S. troops in Iraq than he is prepared to commit or than the American people are prepared to support.

The war's supporters, including Senator McCain, overlook the inconvenient fact that neither the Sunni Awakening nor the Shiite religious parties advocate, or practice, democracy as we might recognize it. They pretend that Maliki is anti-Iranian while accusing Moqtada al-Sadr of being an Iranian stooge. In this way, they can avoid discussing whether they would commit troops and resources to missions that George W. Bush has long abondoned.

President Bush and the pro-war faction point to material improvement in the lives of Iraqis since Saddam's overthrow (and in particular since the surge) as evidence the war was worthwhile. Critics contest this, pointing to the violence and loss of life to argue that Iraqis are worse off. With the lifting of U.N. sanctions and the six-fold increase in the price of oil since 2003, the material quality of life for most Iraqis has improved. And, since 80 percent of Iraqis are either Sunnis or Kurds—two groups brutally repressed by Saddam Hussein—it is possible to argue that most Iraqis are better off in noneconomic ways as well. Thanks to the U.S. invasion, the long repressed Shiite majority won the freedom to determine Iraq's future, and they voted freely to empower pro-Iranian theocratic parties. This is probably a just result, but not one for which the United States should have fought a war.

The debate over whether Iraqis are better off obscures the fact that, both inside Iraq and internationally, there are winners and losers. The winners and losers have their own perspectives on what President Bush did, and not all the winners are grateful to the United States.

Iraq's Shiites are winners. They *should* thank George W. Bush for all that he has done for them. By toppling Saddam Hussein and holding free elections, he enabled Iraq's religious Shiite majority to take power after eighty years of repression and exclusion. By dissolving Iraq's Sunni-dominated army and firing Baathist bureaucrats, the Bush administration enabled Iraq's Shiite religious parties to place their cadres at the top of Iraq's new security services and in key positions in Iraq's bureaucracy.

Iraq's Kurds are also winners and they *are* grateful to George W. Bush. He destroyed the Iraqi state and put them on the path to independence. Kurdistan is one of the few places in the world where George W. Bush could, in 2008, still win an election. (Albania is another.) He screwed up Iraq and the Kurds love him for it.

Iran is a winner. The Iranians will not thank George W. Bush, but they should. He made it possible for Iran's allies to become Iraq's government and so undermined the United States' credibility internationally that there is little support for holding Iran accountable for its nuclear activities.

Iraq's Sunni Arabs are losers. Until the Bush revolution of 2003, Sunni Arabs ruled Iraq. Not all Sunnis supported Saddam Hussein, but almost all Sunnis oppose an Iraq ruled by Shiite religious parties. The Sunni Awakening takes U.S. cash but has no gratitude toward George W. Bush. The relationship with America is an alliance of convenience that will end when it is no longer convenient.

Secular Iraqis are losers. Arabs of a certain generation and class remember a time when it never mattered who was a Shiite, Sunni, or Kurd. Iraqis lived together, friendships crossed ethnic and sectarian lines, groups intermarried, and, they recall, no one knew or cared who was a Sunni, Shiite, or Kurd. This attractive vision of an Iraq past was seductive both for the Bush administration and for many American Iraq experts. It matched American values of diversity, and meant ethnic and religious differences did not have to be part of the planning process in Iraq. For Iraq's business and professional elite, this secular and harmonious pre-Saddam Iraq really existed, although perhaps not as wonderfully as in the recollection. Merchants, lawyers, engineers, and top civil servants really did live lives that crossed sectarian and ethnic lines. The rest of Iraq was, and is, separated into distinct communities of Shiites, Sunnis, and Kurds. And while many Kurds who lived in Baghdad in that pre-Saddam era also recall a vibrant, liberal and diverse city, they all thought of themselves as Kurds, not Iraqis.

What once existed is now gone. Five years of sectarian conflict has destroyed Iraq's once-mixed neighborhoods and made each community more distinct geographically. Iraqi Arabs who did not think of themselves as Shiites or Sunnis now do. What happened is a tragedy, but it happened and cannot be erased. Yet, in spite of all this, many secular Iraqis remain grateful that United States intervened to remove Saddam Hussein.

Whatever Iraq once was, today it is lines on a map inhabited by distinct ethnic and sectarian communities. It makes no sense for Americans to speak of Iraqis* when most of the popu-

---

* Imprecision in language obscures reality and leads to poor policy choices. Refugees provide one example. Two million Iraqis have left their country since the war began, imposing an overwhelming burden on Jordan and Syria, the two countries that have taken the largest number. This number is cited as an indicator of the enormous human cost of the Iraq War and implicit is the notion that refugee flows out of Iraq could get much worse if the war continues. But there is never any discussion as to *who* the refugees are. In fact, most of Iraq's two million refugees are Sunni Arabs. This approaches 30 percent of Iraq's Sunni Arab population and has profound political implications. But, with other groups, the situation is very different. Kurds are returning to Iraq from exile in Iran and, in some cases, Europe. While some Shiites have fled mixed neighborhoods in Baghdad and in Diyala Province for abroad, most have relocated to Shiite neighborhoods in Baghdad and to Iraq's south. Any Shiite exodus out of Iraq is largely offset by Shiites returning from Iran. Refugees are a Sunni problem and need to be addressed as such.

The U.S. military talks about building up the Iraqi security forces, and often cites growing numbers as a metric of progress. But, it matters greatly

lation acts as Kurds, Sunnis, and Shiites. Iraq's distinct communities should be central to future U.S. Iraq strategy, not an afterthought that is wished away.

For the purposes of this analysis, I propose to discuss Iraq strategy in terms of its impact on five geographically distinct parts of the country:

1. *The Shiite south.* This region includes Iraq's second city, Basra, and the Shiite holy cities of Najaf and Karbala. It has Iraq's only outlet to the sea and its large oil fields are estimated to include 80 percent of Iraq's proven reserves and 70 percent of its current production. The south is overwhelmingly Shiite, although Basra once had a significant Sunni population in the city center and in nearby Zubair. SIIC, which favors creating a super Shiite region (akin to Kurdistan), controls six of the nine governorates, including Najaf and Karbala. Moqtada al-Sadr, who opposes a southern region, controls two governorates. With its oil, its port, and its large population, Basra Governorate is southern Iraq's most desirable real estate. Fadhila, a Shiite party that follows the line of Sadr's murdered father, is Basra's largest and would like the governorate to be its own self-governing region. SIIC and the Mahdi Army compete with Fadhila

---

who makes up the security forces. More mutually hostile Shiite and Sunni units may make Iraq less stable. Kurdish battalions inflate the number of Iraqi troops, but they would never follow an order from Baghdad that went against the wishes of their regional government. It is even less useful to talk of Iraqis in the context of a political solution for the country, although this is precisely what most American policy makers do.

for influence in Basra—often violently—and for control over lucrative oil smuggling.

2. *The Sunni center.* This comprises the three Sunni-majority governorates of Anbar, Salahaddin, and Nineveh. The Sunni Awakening controls Anbar, which is 98 percent Sunni, and Saddam's home governorate of Salahaddin. Nineveh, which includes Iraq's third city, Mosul, is more mixed. Mosul is divided by the Tigris into a Sunni west bank and a mostly Kurdish east bank. Nineveh's population includes Christians, Yazidis, Shabaks (Kurdish-speaking Shiites), and Turkmens. A part of Nineveh is already legally part of Kurdistan, and the Kurds seek to incorporate additional Kurdish-inhabited territory. But in spite of its large Kurdish population, the Kurds make no claims to Mosul.

3. *Kurdistan.* This is the territory controlled by the Kurdish political parties since 1991 and recognized as the Kurdistan region under Iraq's 2005 constitution. It consists of Dihok, Erbil, and Suleimania governorates as well as parts of Nineveh, Kirkuk, and Diyala.

4. *The disputed areas.* The principal dispute is between Kurdistan and Arab Iraq over Kirkuk and other Kurdish-inhabited lands beyond Kurdistan's current borders. Shiites claim a part of Anbar for Najaf Governorate, in a dispute that could further fray relations between the two communities.

5. *Baghdad.* Iraq's capital is divided between a Shiite east and a Sunni west, with some Sunni neighborhoods east of the Tigris and some Shiite neighborhoods in the west. Baghdad's population was probably 60 percent Shiite and 40 percent Sunni in 2003. After three years of civil war, the city is appreciably more Shiite. The Sunni Awakening now dominates most Sunni neighborhoods while Moqtada al-Sadr's

main political base is Sadr City, the sprawling Shiite slum that was renamed for his murdered father in April 2003 (it had been Saddam City).

To complicate matters further, the Shiites, Sunnis, and Kurds are internally divided. In 2007 and 2008, the Sunni Awakening fought al-Qaeda (and related Salafi jihadis) in battles that continue. SIIC and Dawa are using their control of the Iraqi Army and national police to suppress Moqtada al-Sadr's forces in Sadr City and Basra in advance of governorate elections that could tip control in Baghdad and some southern governorates away from the ruling parties. In addition, the Badr Organization, SIIC's militia, has fought the Mahdi Army in Najaf and Karbala. In the mid-1990s, the two main Kurdish parties fought each other in a four-year civil war. In this decade, however, the KDP and PUK have put their differences aside to form a unified government in the Kurdistan region and to take common positions in Baghdad. The politburos of the two parties meet regularly to coordinate positions and this Kurdish unity has been a major factor in Kurdistan's successes.

Divisions within Iraq's main communities have not led to cooperation across sectarian or ethnic lines, except in limited circumstances. Even when they fought each other, the Badr Organization and the Mahdi Army both ran death squads that have killed thousands of Sunnis. While Moqtada al-Sadr and the Sunni political parties have a common policy position in favor of a unitary Iraq, they are the factions that hate each other the most. The main cooperation across ethnic and sectarian lines is between the Kurdish alliance and SIIC. The Kurds calculate that supporting Shiite self-government maximizes their own autonomy and prospects for eventual independence, and there is a longtime friendship between the Hakim and Barzani families.

Most experts now recognize Iraq's deep sectarian and ethnic divisions. Politicians, however, come to different conclusions about strategy, and this is a defining issue in the 2008 U.S. presidential election. Republican presidential nominee John McCain accuses his Democratic rival, Senator Barack Obama, of wanting to surrender. McCain advocates staying on a course to victory, which objective he once said might keep U.S. troops in Iraq for one hundred years. In May 2008, he expressed the hope that troops would be out by the end of his first term in 2013. Obama, who won the Democratic nomination in part because of his early and consistent opposition to the war, favors a phased withdrawal of U.S. troops starting immediately after his taking office. Many antiwar activists favor an immediate withdrawal.

Policy makers and experts are divided on the political settlement that might provide the greatest stability in Iraq during and after a U.S. withdrawal. Many experts believe the way to stabilize Iraq is to strengthen the central government. They urge amending Iraq's constitution to reduce the powers of the regions and to give Baghdad exclusive control over oil revenues; incorporating Shiite militias, the Sunni Awakening, and the Kurdistan peshmerga into the Iraqi Army and police, or disbanding them; and working with Maliki's Baghdad government to make it more representative and to extend its authority across the country. Most "centralists" now recognize that Kurdistan is a special case, and they do not propose diminishing Kurdistan's existing autonomy.

The opposing view is commonly—but not entirely accurately—described as partition. Senator Joseph Biden, chairman of the Senate Foreign Relations Committee, Leslie Gelb, president emeritus of the Council on Foreign Relations, and I were among the earliest advocates of a three-state solution. We believe Iraq will be more stable if each of its communities has its own region with a federal government retaining only minimal powers. This is the position Iraqis took in their 2005 constitution (approved by 79 percent of the voters in a referendum). Senator Biden and Senator Sam Brownback offered a resolution supporting the three-state solution that was adopted by the U.S. Senate, 75–23. Democratic Presidential contenders Hillary Clinton, Christopher Dodd, and Biden voted for the resolution. Obama missed the vote but had previously expressed support for the Biden plan. McCain also missed the vote but is a centralist who opposes a three-state solution.

The Bush administration says it supports a stronger central government but has ended up promoting partition. In 2005, then U.S. ambassador to Iraq Zalmay Khalilzad brokered a constitutional bargain that stripped the central government of most of its powers (as compared to the interim constitution) and provided legal authority for regions to veto federal legislation and have their own armies. In 2007, General Petraeus began funding the Sunni militia and helping it take control of Anbar and the Sunni parts of Baghdad.

Senator John McCain, the 2008 Republican presidential candidate, has become the leading proponent of staying the course. According to his campaign Web site, "John McCain believes it is strategically and morally essential for the United States to support the Government of Iraq to become capable of governing itself and safeguarding its people." He shares George W. Bush's goal of "a stable, prosperous, and democratic state in Iraq that poses no threat to its neighbors and contributes to the defeat of terrorists," and he wants Iraq to be "a democratic ally."

He would keep U.S. troops in Iraq until that goal is achieved. He specifically warns that "Iraq must not become a failed state, a haven for terrorists, or a pawn of Iran," which he says are "likely consequences of America's failure in Iraq."

McCain does not question the character of the Iraqi government whose success he considers "strategically and morally *essential to the United States.*" (Emphasis added.) He can't because his entire strategy depends on the Iraqi government being something different from the sectarian Shiite institution that it is. A prime minister put into office by the votes of radical cleric Moqtada al-Sadr probably does not share Senator McCain's view of democracy.* A government whose Interior Ministry ran death squads is not likely to win the trust of the Sunni Arabs it had been targeting. Kurdistan will not let any Iraqi government exercise authority in Kurdistan. And a government comprising political parties long supported by Iran probably is not, as McCain hopes, going to stand up to the Islamic republic.

McCain's strategy is not feasible because it ignores the realities of Iraq divided among Shiites, Sunnis, and Kurds. He says, for example, that "a key test for the Iraqi government will be finding jobs in the security services and the civilian sector for the 'Sons of Iraq' who have risked so much to battle terrorists." The Sons of Iraq, a part of the Sunni Awakening, are Baathists whose agenda is to overthrow Iraq's Shiite government. The Iraqi government will not turn its security over to the Sons of Iraq, who would not loyally serve a government they see (rightly) as sectarian and pro-Iranian. Even if some cosmetic agreement

---

* Maliki won the nomination of the Shiite parliamentary caucus (which was tantamount to election) by one vote in 2006. Nearly half his votes came from parliamentarians loyal to Moqtada al-Sadr.

were reached for the government to hire the Sons of Iraq—and so far the Iraqi government has not delivered on promises to employ Sunni militiamen—it would guarantee neither security nor peace. McCain's strategy for Iraq suffers from all the flaws of the Bush strategy, because it is the Bush strategy.

Other strategies do not have the ambitious goals of President Bush or Senator McCain. They recognize that the United States has interests more important than Iraq and that the Bush administration's goal of a unified, democratic, and stable Iraq is unattainable. These strategies look at Iraq not simply as a whole, but as regions and ethnic/sectarian communities.

If U.S. troops do not have a unified and democratic Iraq as their mission (and as noted, even George Bush has given up on this), then what mission do they have in the country? I can identify four: first, to defeat al-Qaeda; second, to prevent Iran from further extending its influence in the country; third, to protect America's Iraqi allies; and the fourth, to limit, where possible, the Sunni-Shiite civil war. Clarity about the U.S. mission in Iraq should inform the debate about the speed of withdrawal. Where U.S. troops have no feasible mission, there is no need for a continued presence. Where there are still missions to be accomplished, the withdrawal might be more gradual. Barack Obama has proposed withdrawing one combat brigade per month; I support this approach, which has the virtue of getting U.S. forces out while buying time to accomplish some of the steps below.

As noted in chapter 2, the surge has undermined Iraq's unity by establishing a Sunni militia. But, the Sunni militia has accomplished important U.S. objectives by defeating al-Qaeda (and its allies) in Anbar, Salahadin, and west Baghdad. The United States should now have one goal in the Sunni areas of

Iraq: to ensure that the Sunni Awakening remains opposed to, and stronger than, al-Qaeda. The Awakening is, as discussed, comprised of Baathists, many of whom were the backbone of the anti-American insurgency. Americans should be careful, as President Bush and Senator McCain have not been, not to mistake them for friends. The Awakening could turn against the Americans, who were only recently the enemy. It could also end up fighting the Iraqi government, especially if its salaries are not paid or if the army tries to dislodge the Awakening from the places it now controls. In either circumstance, the Awakening might resume the Baathist alliance with al-Qaeda that characterized the early years of the insurgency. Or, if the Awakening is defeated, al-Qaeda could fill the void. The United States faces a dilemma. The longer American troops remain in the Sunni areas, the greater the danger of renewed conflict with the Sunnis. On the other hand, if the United States withdraws, it will not want the Iraqi Army moving in and triggering full-scale war between the Awakening and the Shiite government.

Since there is no meaningful prospect for integrating the Awakening into the Iraqi security structures, the alternative is for the United States to fund the Awakening for the indefinite future. As undesirable as this may be, it is clearly better for Sunni militiamen to fight al-Qaeda than it is for U.S. troops to do so. The United States should reduce its military presence and profile in the Sunni areas while keeping the Iraqi Shiites from undoing the progress made to date.

Iraq's Shiite south includes nine of the country's eighteen governorates and 70 or 80 percent of its oil. In 2008, Iraq's ruling Shiite religious parties (SIIC and Dawa) took a decision to seize control of Basra and parts of Sadr City from the Mahdi

Army and associated radical Shiite militias. Prime Minister Maliki's support for this decision is striking because it put him on the side of SIIC against the Sadrists whose parliamentary votes made him prime minister.

The Iraqi governments military operations had mixed results. Many Shiite Iraqi troops deserted or refused to fight. Some were loyal to al-Sadr and others feared that the Mahdi Army might retaliate against their families. In Basra, Iran helped negotiate a cease-fire that saved the government's face by allowing it to enter the city unopposed but without requiring the Shiite militias to surrender. As a result, Basra is no longer ruled by Shiite extremists who had created a Taliban-style state there, but it is still controlled by religious parties. All factions in Iraq's south are theocratic and none stand for democracy and human rights as expressed in the Iraqi constitution.

President Bush had U.S. troops support Iraqi Army operations in Basra and Sadr City. In effect, he took the side of Iraq's most pro-Iranian political party in an internal Shiite power struggle. He is, in my view, right to prefer SIIC to the more extreme Moqtada al-Sadr. However, this preference does not make it in the U.S. interest to become militarily involved in Iraq's intra-Shiite conflicts. Both sides in the conflict are theocratic, and U.S. troops have no business fighting for theocracy in Iraq. Since the United States has no plausible strategy to diminish Iran's influence in southern Iraq, there is no U.S. interest that justifies a continued U.S. military presence in those areas.

Kurdistan is Iraq's one stable region. Protected by the peshmerga, Kurdistan has been almost entirely free of the terrorism and sectarian fighting that have overtaken the rest of Iraq. Kurdistan's political leadership is dominated, as it has been for decades, by the Barzani and Talabani families, and their close associates. Nonetheless, Kurdistan has come the furthest in developing democratic institutions, including a vigorous parliament, new universities, assertive nongovernmental organizations, and a diverse (but often not very good) media. And, most important, Kurdistan aspires to be Western and democratic. The Kurdistan government is strongly secular and has made a point of empowering women and favoring minorities.

There is no viable "centralist" approach toward Kurdistan. Having secured recognition of Kurdistan's de facto independence in Iraq's constitution, Kurdistan's leaders now jealously guard their region's prerogatives. Nor will Kurdistan voters approve constitutional amendments that diminish Kurdistan's powers. If Iraq's central government is to be strengthened, it will have to be done in a manner that does not apply to Kurdistan.

For the first time in modern history, Kurdistan has nothing to fear from Baghdad. Iraq's president, deputy prime minister, foreign minister, and army chief are all Kurds, and Iraq's Shiite-led government depends on Kurdish support in the Council of Representatives for its majority. The Kurdistan peshmerga is a more capable military force than the Iraqi Army.

Kurdistan does have to worry about its other neighbors—Turkey, Iran, and Syria—all of which are hostile to Kurdistan's de facto independence, and in the case of Iran and Syria, its pro-American orientation. If Iraq collapsed, all three might seek to undermine the one stable and successful part of the country. Without American backing, Kurdistan would inevitably have to turn to one of its neighbors for support and access to the outside world. The Kurdistan government would much prefer that Turkey be that neighbor, and has, as discussed in chapter 4, worked to develop economic and political ties with Ankara.

Historically, however, the Iraqi Kurds have depended on Iran (first the Shah and then the Islamic republic) for outside aid. The Kurds fear that a U.S. withdrawal from Iraq would again make them dependent on Iran.

The Kurdistan government has offered the United States military bases in Kurdistan. Even a small U.S. presence is likely to deter Kurdistan's neighbors from direct intervention. Thus, at relatively low cost, the United States could preserve what has been achieved in the one part of Iraq that turned out as the Bush administration hoped for the entire country. U.S. protection would discharge a moral debt to a people who placed themselves at risk by fighting as American allies in the Iraq War. A U.S. military presence in Kurdistan can also serve U.S. interests in combating al-Qaeda and minimizing Iran's influence. From bases in Kurdistan, U.S. troops could support the Awakening and strike at al-Qaeda directly if the Awakening falters. Being landlocked and surrounded by potentially hostile neighbors, the Kurdistan government has invested billions of dollars since 2003 in airports and long runways. These could be used to re-supply a small U.S. garrison if the security situation falters in the rest of Iraq. The Kurdistan government has offered to have the peshmerga provide security for the Americans, as they do now for a Korean brigade stationed in Erbil.

The disputed areas may be the most volatile part of the Iraqi equation. They have, however, largely been ignored by the Bush administration. As the United States moves toward leaving Iraq, it needs a strategy to contain or, ideally, to prevent the disputed areas from becoming a flashpoint for new conflicts.

Kirkuk is the most complex of Iraq's disputed areas. Kirkuk consists of an ancient city and a surrounding governorate, officially called Tamin, but usually referred to as Kirkuk. Adjacent to the city is the Kirkuk oil field, a "super giant" that went into production in 1932, still accounts for 30 percent of Iraq's oil production (when the export pipeline is not being sabotaged), and has an estimated ten billion recoverable barrels of oil left. The Kurds have long asserted the city and surrounding governorate were part of Kurdistan, and in the 1992 draft of the Kurdistan region's constitution even made Kirkuk their capital. The Turkmens claim to be a substantial part of the governorate's population and the historic majority in the city. Chaldean and Assyrian Christians also have a historic claim to the city. Starting with the production of oil in the 1930s, successive Iraqi governments have encouraged Arab settlement in the Kirkuk region, principally to dilute the Kurdish claim. Almost all the workers in the Kirkuk oil fields were Arabs, fueling Kurdish anger at not benefiting from a resource that most believe belongs to them. Beginning in the 1980s, Saddam Hussein started to "Arabize" Kirkuk's non-Arabs. The Iraqi government pressured Kurds and Turkmens to reclassify themselves as Arabs and expelled those who refused. After 1991, the regime accelerated expulsions across the Green Line that by then divided the Kurdish enclave from the rest of Iraq. To replace Kirkuk's Kurds, Saddam imported Shiites from the impoverished south, giving them land and cash to make the move. These settlers became known as ten-thousand-dinar Arabs.

Today all of Kirkuk's communities feel aggrieved but there is no shared narrative as to what happened and no agreement on how to right the past injustices. The Bush administration knew Kirkuk could be a flashpoint in post-Saddam Iraq but, as with Baghdad, they neither planned to secure the city nor sent enough troops to do so. Because of that handicap, the U.S.

military allowed the peshmerga to take the city as Saddam's regime fell. The peshmerga promptly ended looting in the city
(after having done a little looting themselves) and since then
have kept a very tense place somewhat stable. To their credit,
the Kurds did not engage in tit-for-tat expulsions of Kirkuk's
Arab settlers,* but they did encourage expelled Kurds to return
for the specific purpose of having the Kurdish parties win the
local elections. In the January 2005 local elections, the pro-
Kurdistan list (which included some Turkmens, Christians, and
Arabs) won an absolute majority in the governorate council.
The Kurdistan Alliance also won a majority in the governorate
in both 2005 parliamentary elections, suggesting the governorate would vote to join Kurdistan in a referendum.

Resolving the status of Kirkuk is the top Kurdish priority in
post-Saddam Iraq. As part of the 2005 negotiations on the Iraqi
constitution, the Kurds inserted a provision, Article 140, requiring Iraq to hold a referendum in Kirkuk on its status. Prior
to the referendum, the constitution stipulated that Iraq's government was to facilitate the return of Arab settlers to their previous homes, facilitate the return to Kirkuk of expelled Kurds
and Turkmens, conduct a census, and redraw the governorate's
boundaries to make it more Kurdish by undoing a Saddam

---

* I visited Kirkuk in April 2003 and came across several recently abandoned
Arab villages near a large military base where tens of thousands of Kurds had
been executed in 1987 and 1988. My Kurdish escorts could not—or did
not want to—explain what had happened. It is possible that the residents
of these villages were connected to the base and especially feared Kurdish
retribution. But, these departures—or expulsions—appear to have been the
exception in Kirkuk.

Hussein–era gerrymandering that moved certain Kurdish districts out of the governorate. The constitution set a December 31, 2007, deadline for the referendum, but the Maliki government took none of the required preliminary steps. At the end of 2007, under U.S. and U.N. pressure, the Kurds reluctantly agreed to postpone the referendum.

At the start of 2008, Arab legislators (except for the SIIC parliamentarians) united to oppose Kurdish demands, including the holding of the Kirkuk referendum. If the Kurds see that Kirkuk's status is not going to be resolved, they say they will withdraw from the Baghdad government. They may unilaterally annex Kirkuk, which they effectively control, and they could themselves conduct a referendum. Kurdish leaders have repeatedly said that they agreed to be part of the new Iraq solely only on the basis of the constitution, implying that an Arab failure to implement constitutional provisions on Kirkuk could lead to a Kurdistan declaration of independence.

Kurdistan also claims territory in Nineveh Governorate (around Mosul), Erbil Governorate, and Diyala Governorate that goes beyond what is officially recognized as Kurdistan under the Iraqi constitution. In theory, the Article 140 provisions for a referendum apply to this territory as well, but in fact Baghdad does not contest the formal inclusion in Kurdistan of territory that is Kurdish-inhabited. The Kurds also claim areas with mixed populations and territory that may once have been Kurdish but is no more.*

---

* To complicate matters, Iraq's Christian minority is trying to construct a self-governing Christian region around a group of villages on the Nineveh Plain, east of Mosul. The Kurdistan government supports the Christian claim in the hopes this region might affiliate with Kurdistan. Defining a

While Turkey strongly objects to Kirkuk's inclusion in Kurdistan, it has no legal basis (as most Turks recognize) for telling Iraq how to organize its internal administration. Turkey's intervention would be much more likely if the Kurds act unilaterally—either by annexing Kirkuk and/or separating from Iraq. Some have suggested that the status of Kirkuk and the other disputed territories be deferred to some unspecified future date. This is an invitation to future conflict. Iraq now has an agreed constitutional mechanism to resolve the status of Kirkuk and thus end an eighty-year territorial fight. Before it withdraws from Iraq, the United States should do the Kurds, the Arabs, and Turkey a favor by resolving the Kirkuk question.

Although Mosul is not a disputed territory, the United States will also need to broker a deal on Iraq's third city. The Tigris divides Mosul into a Sunni Arab west bank and a largely Kurdish east bank. In the absence of any reliable Arab security force, the U.S. military has, over time, made the peshmerga its principal security partner in Mosul. The Kurds have resisted the idea of creating a Sunni militia in Mosul, so there is no Sunni force in the city to fight al-Qaeda, which remains strong there. If the United States does not want to leave a Mosul a battleground between the peshmerga and al-Qaeda, it will need to negotiate an arrangement with the peshmerga that will transfer security duties in west Mosul to a local branch of the Awakening.

Iraq's Shiites assert that Saddam drew the borders of Sunni Anbar Governorate in a way that deprived the Shiite Najaf Governorate of large swaths of territory. The land in question

---

territory with a Christian majority requires some very creative gerrymandering and it seems unlikely that the Arabs would accept such an artificially created region.

is desert, but could have oil and gas deposits. Regardless of the justice of the Shiite claim, any effort to take territory from Iraq's embattled Sunnis would certainly lead to a new escalation in violence in Iraq. Iraq does not need a new issue for Shiites and Sunnis to fight over, and the United States should do what it can to keep the Shiites from raising the matter of Anbar's borders.

Baghdad is the front line of Iraq's Sunni-Shiite civil war. The city is divided between Shiites on the east and Sunnis to the west. In 2007, the Sunni Awakening drove al-Qaeda out of most Sunni neighborhoods. This has led to a dramatic improvement in the quality of life as shops, markets, restaurants, and playgrounds have reopened. Music and DVDs, which the staunchly fundamentalist al-Qaeda had suppressed, are now available. Women and girls have greater freedom to work and go to school.

In the Shiite east, the change is less pronounced. Moqtada al-Sadr made a strategic decision not to fight the U.S. surge, but instead have the Madhi Army stand down in place. (Al-Sadr calculated that sooner or later, the Americans would be gone and he wanted to conserve his forces for the battle against the Sunnis and his Shiite rivals.) U.S.-supported Iraqi troops have taken control of parts of Sadr City, but Moqtada is still the major force among the capital's Shiites.

While the surge has helped reduce violence in Baghdad, it has done nothing to close the city's sectarian divide. The reason is simple: real security requires an Iraqi Army and police that operate as neutral guarantors of public security and therefore can be trusted by both Sunnis and Shiites. The United States could not create such a force because there are not many neutral Sunnis and Shiites, and because the last thing Iraq's sectarian Shiite government wants is a neutral security force. In these circumstances, both Sunnis and Shiites will rely on their own forces for protection.

When I wrote *The End of Iraq* in 2006, I saw no role for the U.S. military in Baghdad. I argued that Baghdad's horrific sectarian violence would continue with or without a U.S. military presence and, that being the case, there was no reason to keep troops in Baghdad. All the elements that made Baghdad a front-line city are still there: a geographic division between Shiite east and Sunni west, Sunnis and Shiites relying on their own militias for security, and the absence of neutral Iraqi security forces. But the switch of the Sunni areas from al-Qaeda control to the Awakening and the decline in violence has created opportunities for peace. U.S. forces can help demarcate the respective Shiite and Sunni zones in the capital, work out rules of engagement for the respective militias, and possibly sponsor efforts to professionalize the militias. Over time, it might be possible to stitch the capital together with joint patrols between the militias and the Iraqi Army and police. In 2006, I advocated a rapid withdrawal from Baghdad because there was nothing U.S. troops could do in the capital to stop the civil war. As long as violence in Baghdad remains down, I would make Baghdad one of the last places from which the United States should withdraw.

By looking at Iraq piece by piece, the parameters of a U.S. strategy emerge quite clearly. The United States should withdraw from Iraq because Iraq is a diversion from other more pressing national security tasks. The first place to pull out is from the south. While the U.S. does have favorites among Iraq's Shiite religious parties, it is not such a strong interest as to justify becoming involved in an intra-Shiite civil war. The United States should reduce its footprint in the Sunni areas, consistent with the Awakening taking over security responsibilities.

We should keep our forces the longest in Baghdad. The United States should accord a high priority to resolving the status of Kirkuk and other territories disputed between Arabs and Kurds. Finally, the United States should accept Kurdistan's offer to host a small garrison in that part of the country.

Iraq has already split into an Arab state and Kurdistan. Even the most vehement Iraqi opponents of federalism concede that Kurdistan is a special case. The Bush administration has quietly—and wisely—shelved the idea of strengthening Iraq's central government legislatively or by amending the Iraqi constitution. Instead, U.S. ambassador Ryan Crocker and his team have focused on negotiating bilateral agreements—effectively treaties—between the central government and Kurdistan. Once the issue of sovereignty is set aside, Arabs and Kurds may find they have many practical reasons to cooperate.

Kurdistan does not have a long-term future in Iraq. Almost unanimously, the Kurdish people want their own state. (In a January 2005 nonbinding referendum, 98 percent of Kurdistan's voters expressed a preference for independence). Many Kurds believe—and hope—that the Sunni-Shiite civil war will lead to the collapse of the Iraqi state and thus give them the chance for independence. But increasingly, the rift between Arabs and Kurds is a two-way street. Iraqi Arabs resent the Kurds for their single-minded focus on Kurdistan and their hostility toward Iraq. As a practical matter, the Kurdish attitude has made it almost impossible to pass national legislation. In the end, Iraqi Arabs may decide they are better off without Kurdistan, paving the way to a velvet divorce.

The central problem in Iraq is between Sunni and Shiites. While the rise of the Sunni Awakening may serve U.S. purposes by defeating al-Qaeda, Iraq's Shiites may come to see the Awakening as a greater threat than al-Qaeda. Al-Qaeda is a vicious terrorist organization devoted to killing Shiites but cannot take power in Iraq. The Awakening is a much more organized force that, with outside backing and enough time, could threaten Iraq's new Shiite order.

The Awakening is a ready-made vehicle for Sunni Arab states, including Saudi Arabia, Jordan, and Egypt, to intervene in Iraq's civil war. The Sunni militias do not need arms, with which they are already well supplied, but they do need money. It is easy to imagine Saudi Arabia taking over the financing of the Awakening councils and their militias after—or even before—a U.S. withdrawal. Iran, then, might become even more involved in support of the Shiite central government. In the worst-case scenario, the Iraqi civil war could become part of a wider regional war between the Shiites and the Sunnis.

The Bush administration wants the Iraqi government to integrate the Awakening into the Iraqi Army and police, but it has so far refused to do so. While the Awakening wants the weapons, salaries, and status that come with being Iraqi government units, the Sunni militias do not accept Shiite control. The Iraqi government does not like the Awakening, which it sees as a Baathist fifth column. It is unlikely that the integration will take place and, therefore, another solution needs to be found.

Iraq's constitution allows its governorates to band together to form regions. Regions are entitled to a high level of autonomy (indeed, as in the case of Kurdistan, de facto independence) and to maintain security through a regional army, known as "Guards of the Region." Iraq's constitution also provides that each region is entitled to a share of Iraq's oil revenues in proportion to its population (Kurdistan, as we saw earlier, currently gets 17 percent of the revenues). These revenues could fund the

Awakening without making it dependent on the Baghdad government.

Under the surge, the Bush administration has helped the Sunnis create their army but not the region that might control it. This is an unstable situation. If the Sunnis cannot be integrated into a Shiite Iraq—and they cannot—the logical alternative is for them to exercise their constitutional rights to a region. Unfortunately, Iraq's Sunnis have taken an ideological position against federalism provisions of the Iraqi constitution that they see as a Kurdish-Shiite plot to break up Iraq.

If the Sunnis reject having a region and if the Shiites refuse to include the Sunnis in their new Iraq, then it is likely that Iraq's civil war will continue. It will be a lopsided contest. Iraq's Shiites are three times more numerous than the Sunnis and have, in Iran, a powerful ally. By contrast, the Sunni Arab countries that might support their fellow Sunnis—Saudi Arabia, Jordan, and Egypt—are relatively weak, geographically remote, or both. (While Saudi Arabia and Jordan border Iraq, they are far removed from any populated area. By contrast, Iran is relatively close to all Iraq's population centers except Mosul and Ramadi.) A civil war fought to its conclusion means a Sunni defeat. Already, as much as one-third of Iraq's Sunnis are refugees outside the country. Baghdad has gone from being 60-40 Shiite/Sunni in 2003 to 70-30 in 2008. If the civil war continues, Baghdad could become a purely Shiite city. Sunni Iraq would be reduced to Iraq's western desert, Mosul, and a lot of angry refugees in Jordan and Syria. Over the long term, this could be the greatest catastrophe wrought by George W. Bush's ill-considered war.

A three-state solution—with either a formal or informal division of Baghdad—remains the best way to avoid this result. The United States can encourage the Sunnis to reconsider their opposition to federalism, but, after five disastrous years in Iraq, America does not have much credibility. In the end, the most likely end of Iraq is a two-way division between Kurds and Arabs and the triumph of the Shiites over the Sunnis.

At the end of 2008, the United Nations Security Council mandate permitting U.S. and coalition troops to remain in Iraq expires. The Iraqi government is opposed to any new resolution, which means that a continued U.S. military presence will depend on a bilateral agreement between the Iraqi government and the United States. Congressional Democrats worried that a bilateral U.S.-Iraq agreement could commit the next president to the military defense of Iraq. In a characteristically cavalier fashion, the Bush administration dealt with these objections by asserting that the agreement was not a treaty subject to Senate approval or in the category of agreements otherwise subject to congressional review.

Also characteristically, the administration failed to consider the Iraqi perspective. The Iraqi parliamentary leaders announced that their Council of Representatives would have to approve the agreement. Mindful of its own public opinion, Prime Minister Maliki's government objected to many provisions sought by the Americans, including legal immunity for U.S. troops, U.S. control of Iraqi airspace, and, most importantly, a U.S. right to initiate military operations without Iraqi government approval.

By July 2008, the two sides were at an impasse when Maliki demanded a timetable for the withdrawal of U.S. troops. He then interjected himself into the U.S. presidential campaign by telling the German magazine *Der Spiegel* that "U.S. presidential candidate Barack Obama talks about 16 months. That, we think, would be he right time frame for a withdrawal, with the possibility of slight changes."

The Bush administration had vehemently opposed congressional efforts to set a schedule for U.S. withdrawal from Iraq, arguing that withdrawal must depend on the facts on the ground and that a schedule would give the enemy an incentive to outlast the United States. Maliki's endorsement of the main plank of Obama's Iraq plan undercut both President Bush and John McCain. On instructions from Secretary Rice (and presumably the White House), the U.S. embassy got Ali Aldabagh, Maliki's press spokesman, to say that Maliki had been misquoted. Aldabagh wouldn't issue the statement on his own, so CENTCOM issued it in his name. *Der Spiegel* insisted the quote was correct, and, a few days later, Maliki met with visiting Senator Obama. After according him a reception suitable for a head of state, Maliki again endorsed Obama's timeline for withdrawal, and this time spokesman Aldabagh made a point of saying he meant it. Maliki's statement was especially bad news for John McCain. McCain had baited Obama into going to Iraq, arguing that Obama's position on Iraq had failed to take account of the success of the surge that McCain supported and Obama opposed. Now, the Iraqi prime minister was on record supporting the Obama plan and opposing the McCain plan to keep U.S. troops in Iraq at least until 2013.

Having failed to suppress Maliki's comments, President Bush reluctantly endorsed a "time horizon" of 2010 for a U.S. withdrawal. Condoleezza Rice insisted this was not a schedule or deadline, but it was, in fact, just that.

Some conservative commentators suggested that Maliki had concluded that Obama was going to win and wanted to make good with the next U.S. president. Others suggested that Maliki was playing to Iraqi public opinion and didn't really mean what he said. Inside the administration, Bush loyalists grumbled that Maliki was an ingrate and a disloyal ally.

Maliki is a hard-line Shiite militant who spent more than three decades in exile in Iran and Syria. He has no independent power base and holds office by virtue of being the Dawa party's nominee. Dawa has a history of militancy that includes the 1982 assassination attempt on Saddam in the village of Dujail and a suicide bomb attack the same year on the U.S. embassy in Kuwait. As late as 2002, some State Department officials wanted to exclude Dawa from participating in a U.S.-sponsored Iraqi conference of Iraqi opposition leaders because of its historical links to terrorism. While it would be unfair to link Maliki to an anti-U.S. terrorist act a quarter century before, the Bush administration knew nothing about Maliki before he became prime minister. He was not among the Iraqis trotted out to meet senior U.S. officials, and the State Department even had his first name wrong when he became prime minister. It was always odd for the United States to have invested so much in such an unknown quantity.

As prime minister, Maliki always acted consistently with his Dawa roots.* He now believes that Iraq's ruling Shiite religious parties are strong enough to contain both their Shiite rivals and the Sunnis. As long as U.S. troops are in Iraq, he faces pressure

---

* This was most obvious when Maliki rushed Saddam's execution on December 30, 2006. Saddam had been convicted for killing 142 men and boys from Dujail in reprisal for the Dawa assassination attempt. At the time of his execution, Saddam was on trial for the Kurdish genocide, which took more than 100,000 lives. The Kurds wanted to see the genocide trial completed, but Maliki was intent that Saddam's execution should be Dawa's revenge. In so doing, he acted with complete indifference to the Kurds and other Iraqis who wanted justice for far more extensive crimes. Maliki also bears responsibility for permitting Saddam's hanging to become a lynching with Shiite guards and witnesses taunting the dictator.

to accommodate the Sunnis, and in particular the Awakening. With U.S. troops gone, Iraq's Shiite parties can do as they like. And, if they do run into trouble, Iran is there to help.

Iraq is not an island. It is on the frontier between the Arab and Persian worlds, and borders oil-rich Kuwait and Saudi Arabia, long-time American allies Turkey and Jordan, and junior Axis-of-Evil member, Syria. Iraq has been a factor in the Arab-Israel conflict, participating in the 1967 war, supporting Palestinian terrorists, and, during the 1991 Gulf War, launching Scud missiles on Israeli cities.

President Bush and his allies believed change in Iraq would improve the U.S. position in the region. Before the 2003 invasion, neoconservatives argued that the liberation of Iraq would inspire democratic movements that might topple both Iran's Ayatollahs and Syria's Baathists. Encouraged by Ahmad Chalabi's private assurances, the neoconservatives also imagined that a democratic Iraq might recognize Israel, effectively breaking the back of Arab rejectionism. (In office after the 2005 elections, Chalabi's attitude toward Israel was less friendly.) In recent years, both the Bush administration and the neoconservatives have blamed Iran and Syria for its failures in Iraq.

Iraq War critics have also stressed the international dimension of the conflict. In December 2006, the Iraq Study Group (ISG), a congressionally chartered bipartisan commission cochaired by former Secretary of State James A. Baker and former Indiana Congressman Lee H. Hamilton, began its recommendations for a new Iraq policy with a call for a "new diplomatic offensive" to include dialogue with Iran and Syria, a settlement of the Palestine-Israel conflict on the basis of land for peace, and the return of the Golan Heights to Syria in exchange for peace and normal diplomatic relations with Israel. Only after laying out eighteen recommendations for this external approach to the Iraq crisis did the Study Group turn its attention to Iraq's internal politics and to the role of US combat forces. (Although the report was well received in the media and Congress, President Bush ignored, or did the opposite of, what it recommended. Rather than talk to Iran, he equated negotiation with Iran with appeasement. Where the ISG recommended a drawdown in U.S. combat troops, Bush increased their number. And the Iraqi Kurds and Shiites rejected the ISG's recommendations for internal reform that were mostly intended to strengthen a central government that both groups had voted to emasculate).

Unfortunately, there is no external solution to the Iraq crisis. Iran and Syria are not the source of the conflict inside Iraq and therefore are not part of the solution. (Although the Bush administration accuses both countries of aiding insurgents and extremists, Iran is, as noted, an enthusiastic backer of Iraq's Shiite government, while both Iraqi Prime Minister Nouri al-Maliki and President Jalal Talabani were exiles in Syria, protected and supported by the Assad regime.) Peace between Israel and the Palestinians and Israel and Syria are both desirable objectives, but neither has anything to do with fighting between Sunnis and Shiites inside Iraq. The neoconservatives were wrong to imagine that the road to peace between Israel and its neighbors went through Baghdad; it is equally wrong to think that the road to peace in Baghdad goes through Jerusalem and Ramallah.

Nonetheless, the Iraq War has changed the Middle East, and no analysis of future U.S. strategy is complete without looking at the war's geopolitical impact. We have already seen how the war has strengthened Iran and alienated Turkey. While Syria is a less important player, it has also strengthened that country.

The next U.S. president will have to consider how to deal with a Syria that continues to be at war with Israel, that seeks to control Lebanon, and that is, after Iraq, Iran's closest ally in the region.

A few days after returning from Baghdad in May 2003, I attended a dinner party with a senior Pentagon official. Seemingly oblivious to the disaster unfolding in Iraq, he spoke most of the evening about Syria, leaving the clear impression that Assad was next. In those heady days of "mission accomplished," many Washington hawks spoke freely about regime change in Syria with few considering what might happen if they got their wish.

Syria is a dictatorship with hyperactive intelligence services that suppress dissent both at home and in neighboring Lebanon. Most notoriously, Syrian agents are believed to have engineered the assassination of former Lebanese Prime Minister Rafik Hariri in 2005, one of a string of anti-Syrian politicians and journalists killed in Beirut in recent years. Syria is the most hostile of Israel's neighbors and is on the State Department's list of state sponsors of terrorism, principally because of its support for Palestinian radicals. For all this, the likely alternatives to President Bashar al-Assad may be much worse.

Syria's regime is nominally Baathist, theoretically sharing the same vision of a unified Arab world as Saddam Hussein and his cadres. More relevantly, President Assad and many of Syria's other top military leaders are Alawites, a secretive Islamic sect that many Sunnis and some Shiites consider not to be Muslim. (Like the Shiites, the Alawites follow the line of Ali, the Prophet's son-in-law. They are much more liberal in their interpretation of Islamic texts and injunctions, which is why more orthodox Muslims have questioned their faith. Their claim to be Muslim rests in part on the pronouncements of several prominent Shiite clerics).

Constituting no more than 11 percent of Syria's population, the Alawites have, of necessity, ruled the country with a heavy hand. While brooking no political dissent, Syria's government is resolutely secular. It is also tolerant of other religions, including Christians and Jews (Damascus is one of the few Arab cities east of Tunisia that still has a small Jewish population), and has promoted women in public life.

In such a tightly controlled political environment, it is hard to predict who might replace the current regime, but the strongest opposition comes from the Muslim Brotherhood and other Sunni fundamentalists. In Iraq, the Bush administration changed the regime and handed power (much to the administration's surprise) to Iran's closest allies. It is probably fortunate that the neoconservatives never got the chance to make a revolution in Syria.

There are small signs of change in Syria. Since taking over from his father in 2000, Syrian President Bashar al-Assad has relaxed state controls over the economy, producing a business elite that is more numerous and vastly more wealthy. At the end of 2007, I spent several days in Damascus visiting with some of the business figures. They were Sunnis, Shiites, Alawites, and Christians and, like most of the Syrian elite, had relatives in the United States. At a dinner party that included wives (rare in Iraq and unheard of in many other Arab countries), the business leaders seemed confidant and prepared to discuss any subject—except Syrian politics. At this stage, it is not clear whether economic reforms will lead to political liberalization, but the two often go hand in hand.

Since the 1980s, Syria has had close ties with Iran, which

were, until 2003, based on a shared hostility toward Saddam Hussein. Since Saddam's overthrow, Iran has moved closer to Iraq, and today the substance of the Syria-Iran relationship is a shared fear of the United States. Unlike Iraq's ruling Shiite religious parties, Syria's secular leaders have nothing philosophically in common with Iran's theocrats. Syrian ministers told me that they would like closer relations with the United States. One does not have to approve of Syria's regime to see an opportunity to break the Iran-Syria connection. This, in turn, might diminish Iran's role in Lebanon and possibly create a new opportunity to make progress on a Syrian-Israeli peace treaty. The Israelis think there is such an opportunity. Days after George W. Bush told the Israeli Knesset that negotiations with evil regimes equaled appeasement, the Israelis revealed that they had accepted a Turkish invitation for secret peace talks with Syria. It was measure of the decline in U.S. influence in the Middle East that Turkey was sponsoring talks that, for decades, both Arabs and Israelis had entrusted only to the Americans.

The United States has an interest in reform in Syria and, in spite of neoconservative fantasies, no interest in radical regime change. A more astute U.S. foreign policy might exploit the opportunity to promote reform and to split Syria from Iran. But, any rapprochement with Syria will have to proceed with caution. The U.N. Security Council has established a special court in The Hague to try those involved in the Hariri assassination. If, as many believe it will, the Court indicts high-ranking Syrian officials (President Assad's brother-in-law is one rumored target), the United States will have no choice but to pressure Syria to turn over the suspects. U.N. sanctions against

Syria likely would drive it back into the arms of its one friend, Iran.

The Iraq War was intended to make Israel more secure by eliminating Iraq as a threat and by intimidating Iran and Syria. Instead, Israel finds its strategic position incomparably worse. Most Israeli strategists considered Iran, not Saddam Hussein's Iraq, to be the main threat. After 1991, Iraq did not have a nuclear program but Iran did, and Iran has, as noted, taken advantage of the United States' preoccupation with Iraq to advance significantly its nuclear capabilities. In the 1990s, Saddam Hussein's Iraq was a buffer to Iran but not itself strong enough to threaten Israel. Israelis worry that, once the United States withdraws from Iraq, Iran will be able to use Iraqi territory as a base to attack Israel.

Iran's rise has affected security on Israel's borders as well. In Lebanon, the Iranian-supported Shiite militia, Hezbollah, has increased its power in the country. While Iraq did not, in 2003, have weapons that could attack Israel, Hezbollah does. In the 2006 war with Israel, Hezbollah launched approximately 4,000 missiles into Israel, most of which were supplied by Iran.

The Iraq War did nothing to improve the climate for a negotiated settlement between the Palestinians and the Israelis. Three years after the U.S. troops moved into Baghdad, the Sunni fundamentalist organization, Hamas, won elections for the Palestinian Authority parliament. Hamas refuses to recognize Israel, sponsors terrorism, and is supported by Iran.

Although believing himself to be a friend of Israel, George W. Bush has left Israel far more exposed than it was in 2003. With its nuclear arsenal and conventional superiority, Israel can deter a direct Iranian attack. But, with Iran ascendant, the prospect for a strong Israel living at peace in the region is more remote than at any time since 1993. There is no easy way to undo the damage. While he may not succeed, the next president has nothing to lose by reviving the Arab-Israeli peace process neglected by the Bush administration. Israel might also benefit from reduced tensions between the United States and Syria and the United States and Iran (Iran, it will be recalled, did offer in 2003 to end its support for Hamas as part of a package deal with the United States).

In launching the Iraq War, President Bush and his team were intentionally reshuffling the deck in the Middle East. The next president will be stuck with the new hand, and it will not be an easy one to play.

6

Nationalism and Nation Building

George W. Bush invaded Iraq thinking he was liberating Iraqis and instead encountered Kurds, Sunnis, and Shiites. Sectarian and ethnic identity trumped an Iraqi identity, and the only surprising thing is that the administration was surprised. National, ethnic, and religious identity has been at the center of most recent wars—from Lebanon to Yugoslavia. Identities do not always coincide with lines on a map, but they can reshape the map. Of all the lessons that might be learned from the Iraq fiasco, being better prepared to deal with ethnic conflict and separatism must surely top the list.

Separatism and ethnic nationalism were at the root of Europe's bloody conflicts in the 1990s in Yugoslavia, Chechnya, Georgia, and the Trans-Dniester region of Moldova. Kurdish nationalism has produced decades of conflict in Iraq, Iran, and

Turkey, while Lebanon has been torn apart by conflict among Shiites, Sunnis, Christians, Druze, and Palestinians. In the South Pacific, East Timorese rebels fought with homemade weapons for twenty-four years against the far more powerful Indonesian army and helped win the territory's independence in 1999. Meanwhile, in oil-rich Aceh at the northern tip of Sumatra, rebels fought for decades to create an independent Islamic state, ending with a peace deal that gives the rebels much of the self-government they sought. In Africa, a thirty-year war between the Ethiopian government and Eritrean rebels ended in 1990 with Eritrea becoming independent. A peace agreement between South Sudan and the central government in Khartoum gives the mostly Christian and African south the right to secede from a Sudan dominated by Arab Muslims, a right most expect the South Sudanese will exercise. And, even when separatism is not the direct issue, ethnicity is often a major factor in modern wars. This is true of all of Africa's recent conflicts—Congo, Liberia, Ivory Coast, Angola, and Kenya—and of insurgencies and unrest in Burma, Pakistan, and Nepal.

Ethnic conflict often involves neighboring countries. Serbia and Croatia were principal actors in the Bosnia war while the 1998–2003 conflict in Congo became a regional war involving Rwanda, Angola, Uganda, Burundi, Zimbabwe, Namibia, and Chad. Even when the strife is confined within the boundaries of a single country, the United Nations is often involved in the postconflict settlement, either to put back together a fractured state, as in Liberia or Sierra Leone, or to midwife the birth of a new nation, as in the case of Kosovo, and East Timor. Sometimes a coalition of countries undertakes this nation-building work, as did the United States and its European partners when they implemented the 1995 Dayton Peace Accords, which ended the Bosnia war. In Iraq, the Bush administration decided, without much thought, that the United States could do the nation building all by itself.

Looking ahead for the next few decades, it is likely that more countries will break apart, and that, in at least some instances, the United States will, either with allies or through the United Nations, find itself involved in nation building. Clearly, we will want to do better than we did in Iraq.

When the United Nations was founded in 1945, it had fifty-one members. Twenty years later, the membership nearly trebled as the European countries shed their Asian and African colonies. In the 1970s, a few small adjustments were made to the world map: Bangladesh emerged from the improbable arrangement of a Pakistan with two wings separated by a hostile India, Portugal's African colonies won their independence, the British ended their protectorates over the Gulf principalities and seven of them merged to form the United Arab Emirates, and white Rhodesia became Zimbabwe. The United Nations added twenty members, most of them newly independent island microstates in the Caribbean, South Pacific, and Indian Ocean. By 1981, the world map seemed fixed. Then, starting in 1991, twenty-four new countries emerged in Europe from the demise of the Soviet Union, Yugoslavia, and Czechoslovakia, while one European country, East Germany, disappeared to form a single Germany. Even as late as 1988, no one anticipated that the map of Europe would change so radically in such a short period of time.

Even at the fringes, ethnic nationalism can undermine a multiethnic state. The Baltic republics—Lithuania, Latvia, and Estonia—had less than 1 percent of the Soviet Union's territory and 3 percent of the population, but were the agents of its destruction. Similarly, Slovenia, with less than 10 percent of Yugoslavia's people and territorially the smallest of its republics, undid the larger federation. Multiethnic states often stay together because its constituent peoples see no possibility of independence. Once the door to independence is opened, however, many wish to go through.

The United States has, as a matter of national policy, consistently supported the territorial integrity of existing states and almost always opposed secession movements. The continuation of existing states is invariably equated to stability, even when the state in question is an adversary. Thus, on August 1, 1991, President George H. W. Bush traveled to Kiev with a mission to hold the Soviet Union together. He warned the Ukrainian Rada (parliament) against excessive nationalism. The speech was widely derided as "the Chicken Kiev" speech. Within a month, Ukraine had declared its sovereignty and by the end of the year it was fully independent.

Five weeks earlier, the Bush administration had tried to save Yugoslavia, with incomparably more tragic results. On June 21, Secretary of State James A. Baker flew to Belgrade, where he met with the presidents of Yugoslavia's six constituent republics. He warned that the United States would not look sympathetically on any republic that broke away from Yugoslavia. Four days later, Slovenia and Croatia declared their independence and within weeks the region was aflame in war. Baker's mission did nothing to save Yugoslavia; by June 21, its fate was settled. Croatia and Slovenia had voted overwhelmingly for independence, and neither Croatia's president Franjo Tudjman nor Slovenia's president Milan Kucan could have changed course even if they had wanted to, which they didn't. Serbian president Slobodan Milosevic, however, heard Baker's remarks as a green light to use force to seize as much of Croatia (and then later Bosnia) as he wanted for his project of Greater Serbia.

Although one can understand the short-term calculation that led Bush and Baker to want to save the Soviet Union and Yugoslavia,* it is hard to believe that the continuation of either country was in the interest of the United States, the world, or the peoples of those lands. Nearly two decades later, the Baltic republics and Slovenia are in NATO and the European Union with Croatia soon to follow. Russia has become prosperous and, while it is not an ally, it is not an adversary. And for all the flaws of the Putin era, Russia is far more democratic than the Soviet Union ever was. The tragedy of Yugoslavia is not that it broke up but that it broke up in war.

Even if they had been worth saving, the Soviet Union and Yugoslavia were not savable. George H. W. Bush's policy was not just wrong, it was also ineffective. People rarely reconcile to a state that they do not feel to be their own. In most cases, there will eventually be a day of reckoning. The United States' interest should be in a stable and peaceful outcome. Whether this means separation will depend on the specific circumstances, but it will be a rare circumstance when this means holding a state together by force.

In August 2002, President George W. Bush approved a paper circulated by Condoleezza Rice, then the national security advisor, called "Iraq: Goals, Objectives, Strategy." The United States would, the paper said, "Free Iraq in order to," among other objectives, "Maintain Iraq's unity and territorial integrity."

---

* In both cases, it was the same calculation: to save Soviet president Mikhail Gorbachev. The Bush administration feared that Yugoslavia's breakup would set a precedent for the Soviet Union.

Iraq's breakup is one of the more significant unintended consequences of a war intended to hold the country together. But one might ask why maintaining Iraq's unity and territorial integrity was so important *to the United States* that it was one of the six objectives of a war.* The assumption—shared not just by the Bush administration but by the U.S. foreign policy establishment—is that Iraq's unity is essential for stability and to resist Iranian encroachment and meddling by other neighbors. The proposition bears further examination.

Iraq's previous dictators, beginning with King Faisal and ending with Saddam Hussein, used force to keep the Kurds from breaking away and the Shiites subjugated. Violence led to instability and lawlessness, culminating with poison gas and genocide, that gave Iran opportunities to meddle. More specifically, Saddam's war on the Shiites gave Iran the opportunity to organize, fund, and control Iraq's Shiite political parties. In the 1960s, 1970s, and 1980s, the Kurds turned to Iran for support against Iraq's central government, because no one else would help them. Today, Iraq's ruling Shiite religious parties not only are close to Iran because of its historical support, but rely on Iran to defeat the Sunnis in Iraq's ongoing civil war. There may be tactical reasons to keep Iraq together—notably Turkey's concerns—but there is no obvious U.S. interest in Iraq's unity and territorial integrity. The United States does have an interest that the territory that is now Iraq be stable, but this may be

---

* The others were: eliminating Iraq's WMD, ending Iraqi threats to neighbors, stopping the Iraqi government from tyrannizing its own population, cutting Iraqi links to international terrorism, and assisting Iraqis in creating a democracy.

better accomplished through division. This certainly was the case for the Soviet Union and Czechoslovakia, and arguably, for Yugoslavia.

Worldwide, there are at least twenty independence movements with a chance of success in the next twenty years. In some cases, there is little danger of violence. Denmark and the Faroe Islands have agreed fully that the islands, a Danish dependency in the North Sea, can become independent, but have not agreed on how long after independence Denmark should subsidize the economy of these inhospitable and sparsely populated islands. Scotland, Catalonia, Spanish Basque lands, Piedmont (northern Italy), and the French and Flemish halves of Belgium are possible candidates for independence in the next twenty years. In a Europe with open borders, common laws, and a single currency, this will make little difference. Whether citizens of Spain or an independent state, Catalonians would still travel on a European passport, drive cars with a E.U. license plate, use the euro as their currency, and depend on the E.U. capital, Brussels—not Madrid or Barcelona—to protect the purity of their water, the safety of goods sold in stores, the conditions of work, and even their human rights. Precisely because statehood matters much less in Europe than elsewhere, the dissolution of states is more possible and violence less likely. It is also why these internal developments in Europe are of little consequence to the United States.

Much more problematic are separatist movements in the Middle East and Asia. The Iraqi Kurds are the closest to statehood and therefore, ironically, the least likely to be destabilizing. Pakistan faces an ongoing insurgency in sparsely populated Baluchistan (5 percent of the Pakistani population) but could

come apart if Sindh—the home province of assassinated former prime minister Benazir Bhutto—with 25 percent of the
population is further alienated from a country long ruled, directly or behind the scenes, by a Punjabi-dominated military.
Pakistan has supported Sikh separatists in the Indian part of
Punjab in the past, and India could be tempted to repay the
favor by supporting Sindhi secession. Kashmir, India's only
Muslim-majority state, is contested by both India and Pakistan
(Pakistan controls a small part of Kashmir) but many Kashmiris
would prefer to be part of neither country. Kashmir may have
the world's most dangerous secessionist movement. In December 2001, Pakistani-trained Kashmiri terrorists attacked the
Indian parliament. Had they succeeded in killing the prime
minister and Cabinet (who were supposed to have been in the
parliament at the time of the attack but were not), India's likely
retaliation could have triggered the world's first war between
two nuclear states. Sri Lanka's Tamil Tigers have been fighting
for twenty-five years for a separate state in the country's Tamil
majority north and east. The Tigers were the first terrorist group
to use suicide bombers, killing, among others, former Indian
Prime Minister Rajiv Gandhi. Burma is home to many ethnic
groups and several insurgencies. When the junta collapses—as
some day it will—Burma could become Asia's Yugoslavia.

Secessionism is most likely where one group dominates a
state that contains other national groups, each with their own
geographically defined territory. In the Soviet Union, Russians
dominated a federation where fourteen other nationalities had
republics. In Pakistan, the three smaller provinces—Baluchistan,
Sindh, and Northwest Frontier—resent rule by Punjabis who
are 60 percent of the population. By contrast, India is less

vulnerable to separatism because, while its states generally have an ethnic and linguistic character, no single ethnic or linguistic group dominates India.*

Indonesia, the world's fourth most populous country, is another place where a single ethnic group, the Javanese, is a majority in a nation that has scores of different ethnic and linguistic groups living on more than ten thousand different islands. Religious differences exacerbate the ethnic divide. While Indonesia is nearly 90 percent Muslim, the people in the eastern islands are mostly Christian, and in Papua (the Indonesian half of New Guinea island) much of the population is animist. Bali, Indonesia's premier tourist destination, is Hindu.

When the Suharto dictatorship collapsed in 1998, Indonesia appeared to be on the verge of disintegration. Since then, it has granted substantial legal autonomy to its provinces and made a peace deal with Aceh rebels (who thought the Javanese approach to Islam was too relaxed). Indonesia still faces an independence movement in Papua (where many consider the 1962 Indonesia annexation of this former Dutch colony to have been illegal) and unrest in the Christian eastern islands. Hindu Bali has done well in Indonesia but, in recent years, Islamic terrorists linked to al-Qaeda have inflicted serious damage on its tourist industry with bomb attacks. If the attacks continue, or if Indonesia's Muslim majority imposes dress and alcohol codes

---

* There have been secessionist movements in India, notably among the Punjabi Sikhs in the 1980s, in Kashmir, in the Buddhist state of Sikkim, which India forcibly annexed in 1975, and among the tribes in India's northeast. Nonetheless, with the exception of Kashmir, these movements have never developed the momentum to be a real threat to India's unity.

that threaten Bali's tourism, the Balinese might reconsider their membership in Indonesia. Were it to collapse, Indonesia could produce a dozen or more new states.

The Caucasus is another hotbed of secessionism. In 1996, Russia granted Chechnya de facto independence. Chechen extremists—and some imported Arab jihadis—then attacked villages in adjacent Dagestan and Ingushetia. Russia responded by retaking, and mostly destroying, the Chechen capital of Grozny. While the organized Chechen separatist movement has been suppressed, Chechen terrorists remain capable of spectacular atrocities. Two regions of Georgia, Abkhazia and South Ossetia, are de facto independent, thanks in part to Russian support. The Georgia case illustrates the risky international dimension of separatism. At a NATO summit in Bucharest in May 2008, President Bush tried to win agreement for Georgia to start the process of NATO accession.* He failed, but had he succeeded, he would have committed the United States to the military defense of Georgian territory, part of which is held by Russian-supported separatists.

When the European powers carved up Africa in the nineteenth century, they simply drew lines on a map. Since they were drawn with no regard to the local population, Africa's colonial-era boundaries often placed peoples from different tribes, ethnicities, and languages in the same administrative unit while at the same time dividing peoples from the same ethnicity, tribe, or linguistic group among several colonies. When African states started winning their independence in the late

---

* The summit underscored the steep decline in American prestige under George W. Bush. I can think of no other case where allies at a summit rejected the major proposal of a U.S. president.

1950s and the 1960s, the leaders of the new countries agreed that changing Africa's colonial borders, as illogical as they were, was a formula for chaos and endless conflict.

The problem is that keeping the existing borders may also be a formula for endless conflict. Eritrea fought a thirty-year war for independence from Ethiopia, and the war between Sudan's Arab north and African Christian south lasted nearly as long. Ethiopia and Eritrea have clashed over a disputed border, and relations between the two parts of Sudan remain tense, particularly over the implementation of agreements to share oil revenues, but the situation in both places is less violent than when the independence struggles took place. Somalia is arguably the world's most chaotic place, without a real government since 1991 and a haven for Islamic terrorists as well as pirates and drug lords. But, Somaliland, which is the northern part of the country stretching along the Arabian Sea, is stable, growing economically, and not a terrorist haven. It declared its independence from Somalia in 1991, and has functioned ever since as a separate state—albeit one not recognized internationally. Looking ahead, Africa is certain to be the place where the international community—and therefore the United States—is most engaged in peacekeeping and nation building.

Since the end of the Cold War, the U.S. government, the United Nations, and various academics have studied intently the causes of state failure. After 9/11, this question became more urgent. Terrorism, it was assumed, breeds in the swamp of failed states. If the swamp is to be drained, there is a need for policies that prevent state failure. Research shows a significant correlation between state failure and social ills such as low levels of education, high child mortality, great disparities in income and wealth, and corruption. The United Nations and socially

oriented nongovernmental organizations have used this correlation to argue for more funding to fight global poverty, making
the argument that not only is poverty bad for the poor but it is
a threat to the rich.

But not all failed states are poor. Yugoslavia ranked near the
top of social indices for communist countries. With a few exceptions (Cambodia, Haiti, and North Korea), ethnic conflict
is the heart of most recent state failures. This is not a popular conclusion. Being the creature of the world's existing states,
the United Nations is not inclined to policies and research that
question the rationale for any existing state. U.S. policy makers
have been, as noted, reflexively committed to the integrity of
every nation and rarely ask why this is important to American
interests.

The overriding U.S. interest is in stability and minimizing
violence. Instability and violence create the swamp in which
terrorists thrive. The breakup of states can be violent and produce instability, but, as we see in the case of Iraq, Sudan, and
Somalia, trying to hold them together also produces instability,
violence, and opportunities for meddlesome neighbors.

As with most matters in foreign policy, there is no single
rule for how to deal with separatism. Federal units—republics,
states, and provinces—often have the easiest path to independence, in part because their boundaries are set and they already
have functioning govenment structures. As a matter of law, ju-
rists increasingly accept that such units have a right to secede.
So do some countries. The constitution of the Soviet Union explicitly recognized the right of the union republics to leave the
Union, which they did in 1991. Most Canadians believe their
government would eventually accept an independent Quebec if

the province voted decisively to leave Canada in an unambiguously worded referendum. (Because they lacked a clear majority for independence, Quebec's separatist provincial governments have organized referenda with ambiguously worded questions. The most recent referendum, in 1995, narrowly failed, and most observers believe that, as Quebec becomes more multiethnic, the trend is against separatism.) More generally, in assessing whether a people have a right to secede, one might look to the size of the population, the extent of support for independence, and history. Being victimized because of ethnicity strengthens the moral case for secession. Iraq's Kurds understandably do not want to be part of a country that committed genocide against them in the name of pan-Arab nationalism. On the other hand, Bosnian Serb demands for a separate state deserve no sympathy at all. The Republika Srpska exists as a homogeneous Serb entity only because the Bosnian Serb military expelled Muslims and Croats from its territory, including from many places where these communities were the majority. The architects of this policy are on trial in The Hague for genocide.

While moral and legal considerations are important, each case has to be addressed individually. Tibet has a compelling legal and moral claim for independence. China, however, is the world's second-largest economy, a nuclear power, and a veto-wielding member of the U.N. Security Council. The United States needs Chinese cooperation on a range of global and regional issues. Further, there is no prospect that Tibet will win its independence. This is why it makes sense—as the Clinton administration did—to prod China on human rights issues and to encourage negotiations on autonomy with the Dalai Lama. As a republic within the Russian Federation, Chechnya arguably had a legal claim to independence, But, the international community had no interest in the independence of a small state governed by Islamic radicals that launched attacks on Russian territory.

Nationalism and separatism have produced most of the recent conflicts in the Eastern hemisphere and are likely to do so in the coming decades. As in Iraq, facts on the ground—and not U.S. actions—are likely to determine the outcomes. The United States needs to approach the phenomena pragmatically. The current bias in favor of state continuity makes no sense where this is likely to produce greater instability and violence.

In a world where countries come apart, there will, inevitably, be more peacekeeping and nation-building operations. I participated in two such missions—the American-led effort to rebuild Bosnia after the 1995 Dayton Peace Accords and the U.N. Transitional Administration in East Timor (UNTAET), which administered the territory after Indonesia withdrew in October 1999 until independence on May 20, 2002. I have also observed closely, as described in preceding chapters, the Bush administration's effort at nation building in Iraq.

The Bosnia and East Timor efforts were a success. Thirteen years after international forces entered Bosnia in December 1995, the country is still at peace. Many refugees have returned to their former homes. Bosnians of all ethnicities travel freely around the country with security provided by a substantially reformed police. Bosnia's two entities—opposing sides in the 1992–95 war—now cooperate and, through the central government remains weak, the two entities gave up their right to their own armies (as allowed under the Dayton Accords) in favor of a single national army. And in thirteen years not a single NATO peacekeeper died in hostile action.*

In East Timor, the United Nations took over responsibility for administering a territory that Indonesian troops had devastated. In 1975, Indonesia invaded East Timor, a long-neglected Portuguese colony, and in 1976 formally annexed it. An indigenous movement kept up an armed resistance for twenty-four years and, with the collapse of the Suharto dictatorship, Indonesia agreed to a U.N.-sponsored referendum on the territory's future. Perhaps believing their own propaganda about all they had done for the East Timorese, the Indonesians expected to win the vote. When nearly 80 percent of the East Timorese voted for independence, Indonesian-backed militias adopted scorched-earth policies. At the end of 1999, the United Nations found itself responsible for administering a territory of 800,000 where 80 percent of the buildings had been burned, where all government records had been destroyed, where a third of the population had fled the country, and where not a single civil servant—administrator, policeman, or teacher—was employed.

Two and a half years later, East Timor had an elected government and parliament, a functioning civil service, a newly created and trained police force, and four thousand teachers working in rehabilitated schools. Almost all refugees had returned home, and the U.N., acting on behalf of the East Timorese, had negotiated a treaty with Australia that doubled East Timor's share of

---

* On February 14, 2003, Donald Rumsfeld gave a speech in Manhattan deriding the Clinton administration's nation building in the Balkans. He said the Bush administration would do nothing like it in Iraq, and he was right.

oil and gas in the Timor Sea, effectively doubling the country's GNP.

Neither Bosnia nor East Timor is perfect. Ethnic tensions remain not far below the surface in Bosnia. East Timor is still Asia's poorest country and has had intermittent bouts of instability, including a 2007 assassination attempt on its president, José Ramos-Horta, by a rebellious army officer. But the contrast in outcome with the Bush administration's nation building in Iraq is striking.

In Bosnia and East Timor, nation building was an international effort. Both operations were sanctioned by the Security Council and funded by many countries. The United States contributed one-third of the cost of the Bosnia mission (and supplied one-third of the troops). The U.S. did not supply troops to UNTAET but it did pay 30 percent of the cost as part of its U.N. assessment and provided generous amounts of foreign aid. (Several dozen U.S. troops were in East Timor in a supporting role, but under U.S. command). Although the U.N. acknowledged the United States and Britain as the occupying powers in Iraq, it did so grudgingly, and few countries contributed significantly to the effort. (At first, the Bush administration nation builders did not want the U.N. interfering with their ambitious dreams for remaking Iraq, and by the time they needed help, neither the United Nations secretariat nor other countries wanted to be associated with such an obvious disaster.) Bosnia and East Timor were considerably smaller than Iraq, and this made it easier to mobilize needed military and financial resources. But the physical and human destruction was far greater in Bosnia and East Timor and the reconstruction needs comparably greater. Three factors, I think, explain the difference: security, competence, and local participation.

U.N. troops in East Timor had to contend with Indonesian militiamen infiltrating across the border and some local unrest, but in general the security environment was benign. The Indonesians were gone, and the East Timorese were united in their support of the U.N. mission that was there to shepherd the country to the widely shared goal of independence. In Bosnia, however, the security situation was potentially more perilous. The Serb leaders who had launched the war were still in power in their part of Bosnia when the NATO mission began. NATO's overwhelming force and the projection of competence deterred any Serb thought of renewing hostilities, eventually making it possible for the international mission to remove and arrest those responsible for the war. In Iraq, the United States irreparably lost control of the security environment when it arrived in Baghdad with no thought of preventing the looting.

Security, then, is an essential condition for a successful nation-building exercise and there is generally only a brief window for the foreigners (be it the United Nations or the United States) to demonstrate they are in control.

Of great importance is local participation and ownership. UNTAET was a dream come true for the East Timorese who understood that its sole mission was to prepare them to take over the country they had struggled for twenty-four years to achieve. Sergio Vieira de Mello, the U.N. official in charge of UNTAET, was the best diplomat I ever encountered and quickly established a close and respectful relationship with the East Timorese leaders. Even so, after just six months, East Timorese were harshly criticizing the U.N. administration. We were, the East Timorese charged, not consulting them sufficiently and moving too slowly to place Timorese in key positions in the newly created civil service. (These complaints were for the most part without merit. The Timorese leaders designated Timorese to work with the U.N. and then rarely consulted with their own people. The low level of education in the country meant Timorese needed extensive training before they could take over jobs in the civil service.) Vieira de Mello heard the complaints and asked me to design a new system of government.

We proposed to transfer decision-making power to an interim cabinet in which the Timorese had a majority and where they supervised almost all public servants whether from the United Nations or local. Thus East Timorese ministers could decide when to replace an international civil servant with a Timorese and collectively could decide the country's budget and spending priorities. Having been so empowered, the Timorese almost immediately pulled back from its exercise. They asked that the U.N. have an equal number of cabinet members as East Timorese, and Timorese ministers generally kept their international staff, knowing they would be blamed for a decline in services if an unqualified Timorese took their place. East Timorese now look back on the two and a half years of U.N. administration as the best government they ever had, and President Ramos-Horta recently complained that the U.N. "occupation" had not lasted long enough. The reason UNTAET worked is that the East Timorese controlled the pace of the transition. The contrast with Iraq could not have been more pronounced. While Vieira de Mello treated the East Timorese with respect, Bremer belittled the Iraqis. In the end, UNTAET produced laws and a constitution-writing process that applied throughout the country. Bremer's authority never extended beyond the Green Zone, and his constitutional and lawmaking achievements were mostly fantasies written on paper or existing almost entirely in his own mind.

The major problem in nation building is finding competent international civil servants who can help administer a territory while transferring skills to the local population. Diplomats and professional military men and women expect to serve abroad and in difficult conditions. Civilian administrators do not expect to do such service, are generally not rewarded for it, and may not have the necessary diplomatic skills to match their substantive expertise. There is no easy solution to this deficit.

A skilled diplomat such as Sergio Vieira de Mello can do the politics and can establish policy-making institutions. Both the United Nations and the United States have diplomats who can handle political tasks. In addition, the United Nations has specialists with long experience in some of the technical issues of nation building. These include, for example, an office that designs electoral systems and conducts elections, usually the critical step in a political transition. While otherwise disparaging the United Nations, the Bush administration recognized that its skills—and reputation for impartiality—were essential to the conduct of elections in Iraq. Carlos Valenzuela, a Colombian U.N. official who had been my deputy in East Timor, designed the Iraqi electoral system. George W. Bush often points to Iraqis waving purple fingers (indelible ink to stop double voting) as evidence of the success of his Iraq War. The elections were a success—arguably the unique success of the occupation—and they were the work of the United Nations, not the United States.

The main difference between the U.N. staff and U.S. diplomats is availability. U.N. staff expect to be assigned to overseas missions on short notice. U.S. diplomats have fixed tours, and it is difficult to break them. (It is not that Foreign Service officers do not want to serve in places like Baghdad; many do in spite of the danger and disruption to family life. Transferring an officer to an ad hoc nation-building mission leaves a vacancy in her or his existing job, which—if the officer is good and relatively senior—is an important position in its own right.)

Military officers are more readily available. They spend their careers training for combat and related national security missions. Neither diplomats nor military officers are, however, qualified for the many civilian functions in running a country. It is an unusual diplomat or military officer who has set up and run a police force, created a civil service, hired teachers and designed a curriculum, run an electric grid, set up a central bank, designed a health-care system, established a judiciary, or created a social security system. Yet these were all tasks that fell to the U.N. mission in East Timor, and are, to varying degrees, part of other nation-building missions, including Iraq. In East Timor, the United Nations asked governments to propose suitable people. Some were good and many were not.

The problem is simple. The qualities that make for a good police chief in Lisbon or New York may not be those that serve well in creating a new police force in East Timor and Iraq. Effective police work requires local knowledge (including an ability to speak the local language) and diplomatic skills for work in an environment as alien as Dili or Baghdad. The same points apply, of course, to organizing a civil service, educational system, and the like.

Furthermore, organizations resist outsiders. A German or Arkansan judge who is very savvy politically in his own milieu may find it impossible to get his ideas through the U.N. or U.S. government bureaucracy. But an even larger problem is the difficulty in recruiting good people. For a diplomat or military officer, service in Bosnia or Baghdad is a place to be noticed and therefore career enhancing. (It is no accident that three- and four-star generals running Iraq were colonels and brigadiers in Bosnia and Kosovo a decade earlier.)

There is no comparable career incentive for someone working on domestic issues—education, social security, criminal justice, public utilities, etc.—to serve abroad in nation-building missions. Such service is at best a diversion from a successful career aimed at, for example, becoming a big city school superintendent, and may be seen as eccentric. Pulling an administrator out of his domestic position creates a vacancy that the home organization cannot easily fill. If the position can be filled, there may then be no job for the civilian to return to.

Younger people and those on the lower steps of the career ladder are more easily deployed. They tend to be more flexible personally and are not as established in their careers. But being younger and at a lower level usually means having less experience applicable to the task of nation building. The Bush administration recruited many young people to serve in Iraq, but for the most part those hires had no serviceable skill set. The U.S. military has deployed reservists with relevant civilian skills to undertake nation-building-related assignments in Iraq. Sometimes this has worked well, although some in the military grouse that electricity is not in their job description. At other times, it has been a disaster—most notably when Charles Graner, a reservist who had worked as a corrections officer in Pennsylvania, supervised the treatment of Iraqi detainees in Abu Ghraib prison.

Secretary of State Condoleezza Rice has proposed the creation of a civilian reserve corps that can be deployed on short notice to nation-building missions. While this may meet some needs, it is not a real solution. Unless there is extensive—and expensive—training, the civilians will deploy, as now, without the requisite diplomatic skills. Such a corps will not solve the problem of finding people willing *and able* to leave a successful top-level position at home to create a civil service or police force in a war-torn land.

The United Nations is far better equipped at doing this than the United States government. Even so, finding and deploying the right people was a challenge for the U.N. in a place as small as East Timor. The Bush administration did not even try to find qualified people to run Iraq.

The Bush administration has approached the problem of ethnic nationalism in Iraq by acting (and possibly believing) that it does not exist. It approached nation building in Iraq by thinking it would be easy, so easy as not to require planning or competent people.

Ethnic nationalism and separatism are likely to dominate the headlines for the next twenty years, as they have the last twenty. The American track record in anticipating the phenomena—from Yugoslavia to Iraq—has been dismal, resulting in a long and deadly period while policy makers caught up with reality. It will serve our country and the cause of a more peaceful world if we are prepared. The policies pursued should depend on the specific case, but it is counterproductive to commit America to the unity of states that are beyond saving. The focus should be foremost on ending violence and saving lives.

7

An Effective National
Security Policy

In his terms in office, George W. Bush has been criticized for being too partisan, too divisive, too unilateralist, too much in the pocket of U.S. business interests, and too militaristic. While there may be merit to these charges, they miss the main point. Liberals and conservatives, Republicans and Democrats may disagree on the specifics of U.S. foreign policy: the circumstances that justify the use of force, the role of the United Nations and other international institutions, the extent to which Washington should promote business interests. But there should be agreement on one point: U.S. national security policy should be effective.

George W. Bush's policies have been ineffective. They have not accomplished the goals Bush himself laid out with regard to Iraq, Iran, or al-Qaeda. At the end of Bush's second term, the United States is both unpopular around the world and less secure at home. The reason George Bush has been ineffective is simple. He has substituted rhetoric and wishful thinking for strategy.

Strategy is a plan to apply available resources efficiently to accomplish set objectives. America's resources include money, our armed forces, our diplomats, the support of our allies, and our prestige in the world. Americans generally agree on our broad objectives. Living in a prosperous and powerful country, we want a stable world, which we rightly see as the best guarantee of our physical security and economic well-being. Stability is, as I have argued in the previous chapter, not the same as the status quo. And when we pursue other goals—democracy, free trade, and environmental protection—we do so in pursuit of stability.

In evaluating a particular course of action—such as the Iraq War—we do not need to reach the question of whether it is morally justified if it does not serve the national interest. Liberals and conservatives should equally oppose ineffective policies. The following are some simple steps that can contribute to a more strategic national security policy and therefore a more effective one.

Prioritize National Security Objectives

No country, even the United States, has the resources to do everything. The next president must prioritize U.S. foreign policy objectives according to importance, prospect for success, risks, and costs. In general, the more important the objective, the more resources can be applied to accomplish it and the more risks can be taken. If the most important objective is to prevent the spread of nuclear weapons to rogue states and nonstate actors, then the focus must be on the countries most likely to behave like rogues or most likely to proliferate nuclear technology. Iran might fit into the former category, Pakistan the latter, with North Korea being both a rogue and a proliferator. In pursuing national objectives, the United States has a choice of instruments: diplomacy, foreign assistance, economic sanctions, covert action, and military force. The preferred instrument is always the least costly and least risky, which is usually diplomacy. The more critical the objective, the more justified is the use of risky and costly instruments such as armed force.

Objectives also need to be prioritized against one another. In 2002, President Bush rightly identified the greatest threat to the United States as coming from the world's most dangerous countries with the world's most dangerous weapons. He then turned his focus to a country that, thanks to sanctions and previous military defeats, was not particularly dangerous. (Even if Iraq had hidden chemical weapons, it would have posed a minor threat as compared to rogue states with nuclear programs.) By focusing on Iraq, the Bush administration effectively gave a free pass to North Korea and Iran to move forward with their nuclear programs. With the United States tied down in Iraq, North Korea detonated a nuclear bomb in 2006 and Iran enriched uranium. Preoccupied with Iraq, the administration had neither the leverage nor the attention to focus on the most dangerous proliferator, Pakistan. Furthermore, the fact that the Iraq War went badly greatly strengthened Iran's position in the region, and reduced U.S. options for dealing with the Islamic republic.

Finally, objectives need to be achievable with the resources one is prepared to commit. The flaw with Bush's ambitions for a democratic, unified, and stable Iraq is that it is not achievable with the troops that we have in the country, or any reasonable augmentation of them.

Be Knowledgeable

Bush's approach to Iraq was striking in how indifferent he was to the realities in the country. It is hard to apply resources to a problem or place you do not understand. Political campaigns poll every conceivable demographic subgroup—for example, soccer moms or security dads—and tailor messages aimed at winning that particular demographic. Yet the Bush administration aimed to win in Iraq by treating the place as if it were inhabited by a single people sharing common goals. Many of the administration's critics make the same mistake. When I hear generalizations about Iraqi opinion—for example, that Iraqis resent the presence of U.S. troops—I always ask, Which Iraqis?

Intelligence Is Not the Same As Knowledge

American policy makers rely on intelligence as if it were the gospel. As a government official, I have sat in countless meetings where the phrase "the Agency believes" was used to stop further discussion. However, while the CIA has impressive resources and many good people, intelligence is, by its nature, often partial and subject to different interpretations. Intelligence community judgments are just that: the collective and considered opinion of some smart people. They are not necessarily right.

Secret information is not always better than public information or even ordinary observation. In May 1998, India caught the CIA by surprise when it tested three nuclear weapons. The

CIA had no secret source in the office of India's newly elected prime minister, A. B. Vajpayee, to tell them a test was imminent. But everyone knew that India could make nuclear weapons (it had tested what it called a peaceful nuclear explosive device in 1974) and that it had a test site ready. Vajpayee's party had been in power for thirteen days in 1996, and during that brief period in office, it had been preparing to conduct a nuclear test. Finally, senior officials in Vajpayee's government had said publicly during the election campaign that they would conduct a nuclear test. While the failure to anticipate the India nuclear test is criticized as an intelligence failure, I see it as a failure by our diplomats and other senior officials, who deferred to the CIA on a matter about which they themselves ought to have made judgments.

Obviously, the CIA's assertion that Iraq had WMD was an intelligence failure. But even if Iraq had chemical weapons and a rudimentary biological weapons program—as the CIA asserted—it does not follow that it was the same level of threat as Iran, North Korea, or Pakistan, or that war was the correct strategy for dealing with the supposed WMD. Indeed, once Iraq agreed in 2002 to readmit U.N. inspectors—under threat of war—the United States could be reasonably assured that Iraq did not have a nuclear program or a significant ongoing program to manufacture chemical or biological weapons. (The risk that inspectors would uncover ongoing programs would be too high, even if the Iraqis could conceal some preexisting stocks of chemical weapons, which many, myself included, thought they had.)

Beware of the Herd Mentality

My late friend, Senator Daniel Patrick Moynihan, used to say of the CIA: "They told us everything about the Soviet Union except that it was falling apart."* This was no small point. We spent trillions of dollars combating an adversary that was far less powerful than we imagined. Yet, both in government and among the foreign policy experts, the commonly shared view was that the Soviet Union was an existential threat to the United States.

Conservatives, in a view coherently argued by Reagan's U.N. ambassador, Jeane Kirkpatrick, saw communism as so powerful that, once a country slipped into its grip, the country would never emerge. For this reason, Kirkpatrick urged that the United States strongly support right-wing regimes—such as Chile's Pinochet and South Africa's apartheid regime—because, as bad as they were, the alternative was worse. As a seventeen-year-old high school student studying Russian, I spent eleven weeks traveling around the Soviet Union and Eastern Europe in a VW minibus, staying in campgrounds mostly with Russians. The weaknesses of the Soviet system were apparent, including the poor quality of everything from housing to aircraft to food and consumer goods. And I never met an Eastern European who believed in the communist ideology. What the conservatives saw as evil and threatening, I saw as evil, ineffective, and doomed to fail.

---

* Senator Moynihan did predict the demise of the Soviet Union. Writing in 1980 for a *Newsweek* series on what to expect in the coming decade, Moynihan said the Soviet Union would disintegrate and that the problem would be accounting for its nuclear weapons.

I came away with one other conclusion from my trip to the Soviet Union: that it is impossible to understand a country without being there. In the buildup to the Iraq War, Middle East experts provided the administration and Congress with authoritative advice on a country they had never visited. Not surprisingly, they reinforced one another's preconceptions: that Iraq was among the more secular of the Arab countries; that Iran could not influence Iraq's Shiites because the ethnic differences between Arabs and Persians were far more important than the shared Shiite faith; and that Iraq's Kurds felt a loyalty to Iraq, even as they fought Saddam Hussein. Although some of these experts had studied Iraq far more systematically than I ever did, these conclusions did not match what I had observed in a country that I visited many times.

As currently structured, the foreign policy community—both in government and on the outside—has a strong bias toward the conventional wisdom. Outliers are not appreciated in a system where there is no penalty for being wrong. In the 1980s, government intelligence analysts and foreign policy professionals did not consider whether the Soviet Union was a potential failed state. It was accepted that the Soviet Union was a powerful and enduring superpower, and everything was interpreted through that lens. Looking for evidence of Soviet power, analysts found it. At one point, the CIA even concluded that East Germany's per capita GNP exceeded that of West Germany's, overlooking the fact that there were not many Germans trying to cross the wall west to east. To suggest that the Soviet Union was not a threat because it would soon fall apart might not have been a firing offense but it was certain to ensure irrelevance, which for most professionals was a far worse fate.

Being wrong is costly. In the 1980s, we went nearly two

trillion dollars into debt to finance a defense build-up to combat an adversary that was on the verge of collapse. We also besmirched our ideals in search of allies against the Soviet Union, supporting apartheid South Africa, South American dictators, Afghan fundamentalists, and Saddam Hussein. The Afghan fundamentalists facilitated the deadliest attack ever on American soil, and the United States ended fighting two wars against erstwhile cold-war ally, Saddam Hussein. While many foreign policy experts had reservations about the 2003 Iraq War, few dared challenge the conventional wisdom that Iraq was a nation, and those who did were mostly dismissed until proven right.

Being conventional is the path to respectability in U.S. foreign policy circles both inside government and outside. But, what we need are keen observers who reach common sense conclusions that they are not afraid to articulate.

Diplomancy Is Worth Several Divisions

For the last four decades, the United States has generously funded the military while usually starving the State Department and foreign assistance programs. In the 1980s and 1990s, the U.S. Congress even refused to pay the full U.S. assessments to the United Nations, even though the United States made more use of the U.N. than any other country. Funding for all U.S. government international operations—the State Department, foreign assistance, U.N. contributions, and international broadcasting—is less than 10 percent of the Pentagon budget, yet these programs are almost always the first cut in the name of budgetary austerity.

The U.S. military pays a steep price for this misallocation

of resources. In Iraq, soldiers undertake tasks that more appropriately should be done by qualified diplomats simply because there are not enough diplomats available. If the Coalition Provisional Authority had been more professionally staffed, the occupation would have been more competently managed and the military mission in Iraq might today be less costly and less perilous. (Of course, the ideologues running CPA would have had to have listened to the professionals.)

The United Nations is the tooth to most conflict prevention, peace-making and nation-building exercises. The U.N. staff includes the people on the ground who interact with the warring factions, negotiate agreements large and small, and facilitate most international movement from the delivery of humanitarian supplies to the movement of diplomats. During the Croatia and Bosnia wars, the United Nations deployed more than 30,000 troops to police cease fires, protect safe areas, and deliver humanitarian supplies. In many aspects, the mission was a disaster. Dutch peacekeepers stood aside as Serb forces overran the Srebrenica safe area and massacred more than 8,000 men and boys. Most of the U.N.-negotiated cease-fires crumbled, some within minutes of being signed. In the end, it took American military intervention in the form of NATO bombing and robust U.S. diplomacy to bring peace. And yet, we could not have negotiated the Dayton or Erdut peace agreements (the treaties that ended the Bosnia and Croatia wars) without the United Nations. As the Croatia peace negotiator, I physically could not have reached rebel Serb territory without U.N. logistical support to cross the front lines. But, the United Nations did much more. U.N. personnel knew the actors and the issues and were able to provide essential support to the negotiations. In the early days of the Bosnia peace shuttle, the Holbrooke team needed U.N. support to get into besieged Sarajevo. And, for its multiple shortcomings, U.N. humanitarian operations kept Sarajevo alive through a siege of more than 1,000 days, ensuring there were people still alive who might benefit from the peace.

The U.N. Security Council often sends U.N. missions into conflict zones because Council members, including the United States, are unwilling or unable to take more decisive action and yet feel they need to do something. Not surprisingly, a large number of these missions fail to produce results. But, almost invariably, if and when there is a prospect for peace, the United Nations will be part of it. In Iraq today, the United Nations is at the forefront of the diplomatic effort to resolve the status of Kirkuk and the other disputed areas.

At the beginning of the decade, I taught national security strategy at the National War College in Washington, D.C. My military students were colonels or lt. colonels, or their equivalents, from all services. Many had served in the Balkans in the 1990s and would go on to serve in Iraq. When presented with a strategic problem, they would invariably call for diplomacy, more foreign assistance, and a greater U.N. role. When asked where to get the money to pay for these activities, they would invariably point to the Pentagon budget. These men and women serving on the ground in combat situations understood that the military needs more than the best hardware and training. So, why don't decision makers in Congress and the administration understand this as well?

When I worked for the State Department and the Senate Foreign Relations Committee, the standard explanation was that there is no domestic constituency for foreign programs.

Retired diplomats tried to create such a constituency by telling their congressman that they existed and by explaining the important work diplomats did. Predictably, these efforts fell flat.

The real reason that U.S. diplomacy is underfunded is that neither presidents nor secretaries of state fight for more resources. When the secretary of state goes to Capitol Hill, senators and representatives want to talk about U.S. foreign policy and not budgets. When she meets with the president, they talk about foreign policy, not resources. By contrast, both within the administration and on Capitol Hill, secretaries of defense focus significantly on budgets, weapons systems, and personnel. To their credit, Secretary of State Colin Powell and President Bush used 9/11 to secure a major augmentation in diplomatic resources to go along with the military build-up. The next president and secretary of state must make diplomatic resources a major priority, along with the content of foreign policy. It might help if the president and the secretaries of state and defense presented a unified national security budget rather than continue the outdated and now artificial distinction between diplomatic and military resources.

If U.S. diplomats are to be effective in conflict zones, they need to be able to do their jobs. The Bush administration has trumpeted the Provincial Reconstruction Teams (PRTs) in Iraq as a key component of its reconstruction and reconciliation strategy. With a team for each of Iraq's eighteen provinces, the PRTs are meant to coordinate with local officials to ensure the effective spending of U.S. reconstruction funds, to report on the local scene, and to make diplomatic representations. They are, however, so burdened by security regulations that they can rarely leave their compounds and are, for the most part, ineffective. In January 2007, I visited the PRT in Erbil. It was locked up in a one-block compound. The PRT officer responsible for Suleimani Governorate had been in Iraq nearly a year and had been to her province just twice. Suleimani is one of the safest places in Iraq (I usually travel there just with a driver), and the Kurds had offered to provide security. The State Department's office of diplomatic security, however, insisted on the same rules for all PRTs (regardless of danger) and applied the same rules to safe Kurdistan as to then very dangerous Anbar.

In recent years, every diplomat serving in a war zone (Croatia and Bosnia in the 1990s, Iraq and Afghanistan today) volunteered to go. They are well aware of the dangers but willing to take the risk because these are the places where diplomats can accomplish something. Almost all diplomats I met serving with the PRTs were willing to take greater risks to do their jobs. During the Croatia and Bosnia wars, I sent embassy staff into combat zones in Croatia and Bosnia on a regular basis. The embassy staff uncovered atrocities and gained access to Bosnian Croat–run prison camps. Using this information, I was able to get the Croats to release more than 5,000 Muslim prisoners from inhumane confinement and to push for an end to the atrocities, setting the stage for a peace agreement between the Muslims and the Croats. Everyone who went into Bosnia volunteered to go (and very much wanted to go), and before each trip, I carefully reviewed the security situation. We were prudent, and perhaps lucky. No one got hurt, and we accomplished important U.S. government goals. If we had operated under the rules applied to U.S. diplomats in peaceful Kurdistan, we would have accomplished nothing.

We routinely ask our military to put their lives on the line in pursuit of national security objectives. It is absurd to stop U.S.

diplomats from voluntarily taking a fraction of the military's risk to accomplish the same goals.

Public Diplomacy Is a Tool of Limited Value

All administrations complain that they are misunderstood abroad. This has led to an enormous investment in what is called public diplomacy: Voice of America broadcasts, surrogate radio and TV stations,* press activities, tours for foreign opinion leaders, and educational exchanges. In its early years, the Bush administration hired an advertising agency to produce Arabic language commercials showing Muslim families living contented lives in the United States. And, in Iraq, the U.S. government spent millions trying to persuade Iraqis as to how much the CPA was doing for them and of the glories of the American-written interim Iraqi constitution.

The premise of these activities is that the more foreign-

---

* Surrogate radio and TV stations employ nationals from a country to broadcast into the country. It is the surrogate for the free media that the country does not have. During the Cold War, the U.S. government funded Radio Free Europe and Radio Liberty to broadcast into communist Eastern Europe and the Soviet Union. They proved so popular that when the iron curtain fell, the Czech Republic invited the stations to set up shop in the parliament building for the defunct Czechoslovakia on Wenceslas Square in Prague. Today the United States does surrogate broadcasting to Cuba, Iran, and the Arab world. The Arab language broadcasts include a satellite television channel, TV Hurra ("the free one"), and Radio Sawa, which broadcasts pop music and news with a pro-American slant. TV Hurra has to compete with scores of state and private Arab language channels, is not considered interesting, and has a small audience. Radio Sawa does somewhat better, perhaps because there is less competition on the FM band.

ers know about us, the more they will like us. But, most foreigners—including in the Middle East—know a lot about the United States and its policies already. Middle Eastern elites frequently visit America and/or have relatives in the country. Many ordinary Middle Easterners do see the United States as a violence-prone, promiscuous land, an image America created for itself through its export of Hollywood movies and television programs.

For the most part, people in the Middle East—and much the rest of the world—take a dim view of the United States because of our policies. This is not because they do not understand our policies but rather because they *do*. Arabs see the United States as pro-Israeli and as indifferent to the suffering of the Palestinians because it is pro-Israeli and because the Bush administration—in sharp contrast to its predecessors—has made no effort to advance the Middle East peace process. The Iraq War has done incalculable damage to the U.S. reputation around the world not because foreigners don't understand our reasons for invading but because they see—completely accurately—that we invaded Iraq to eliminate WMD that we insisted were there but that did not exist.

Good public diplomacy is not primarily a matter of explaining America and its policies better; it is a matter of having better policies. U.S. prestige in the Islamic world was at an all-time high during Bill Clinton's presidency. Partly this is because the Palestinian-Israeli issue was less prominent after the signing of the Oslo Accords (on the White House lawn in 1993) and significantly because the United States was seen as the champion of the Bosnians at a time when the Europeans (who are traditionally seen as less pro-Israel) appeared unwilling to help a

Muslim people. When the Palestinian uprising started in 2000, President Clinton did not sit on the sidelines but actively pursued a comprehensive peace deal that almost worked.

The Less Said About the Freedom Agenda the Better

George W. Bush began his second term in office by declaring, in the opening paragraphs of his inaugural address, that "It is the policy of the United States to seek and support the growth of democratic movements and institutions in every nation and culture, with the ultimate goal of ending tyranny in our world." While the United States has been promoting democratic movements at least since the end of World War II, Bush has carried the rhetoric of freedom, rule of law, and diversity to a new level in presidential discourse. And, since 2001, the United States has spent $7 billion on democracy programs, not including money spent in Iraq.

It is time to cool the rhetoric. The United States is, of course, a great democracy, but it is not necessary to proclaim this all over the world. Non-Americans do not imagine that they are so deficient as to need an American lecture on freedom. Guantánamo and Abu Ghraib have hurt the American brand abroad, but so have the internal shortcomings of American democracy. For many foreigners, the 2000 election was a real shock. The American political system produced an outcome where the candidate with fewer votes became president and where election officials in Florida operated not as neutral arbiters of the balloting but as partisans. But the greatest damage was done by the U.S. Supreme Court decision in *Bush v. Gore*. It is hard to take seriously American lectures on rule of law when Supreme Court justices decide a presidential election on the basis of their personal partisan preferences. Rule of law exists when laws are applied impartially. Foreigners do not believe the five justices who selected Bush would have reached the same conclusion if the roles of Bush and Gore had been reversed.

In 1983, the Congress created the National Endowment for Democracy and international institutes associated with the Democratic and Republican parties. When they run programs in foreign countries, these institutions use experts and politicians from all over the world. The United States will be more effective in promoting democracy if it does not always do so with an American—or even western—voice. And, it will help to acknowledge and fix some of the deficiencies of the American democratic system.

Negotiation Is Not Appeasement

On the occasion of Israel's sixtieth anniversary, George W. Bush used a speech to the Knesset to interject himself into the U.S. presidential campaign. Without naming the Democratic presidential nominee, he compared Barack Obama's willingness to negotiate with Iran to British Prime Minister Neville Chamberlain's appeasement policy toward Hitler. And, in case anyone missed the comparison, he quoted a U.S. senator (Republican William Borah of Idaho) who said, following Hitler's invasion of Poland, "If only I had had a chance to talk to him." The speech was remarkable in many ways. First, it went against a long tradition of presidents not using foreign venues for partisan purposes. Second, the speech continued the Bush White House tradition of getting its World War II history wrong.* Chamberlain did not appease Hitler by negotiating with him, but rather by forcing Czechoslovakia to cede the Sudetenland to Germany. Indeed, had Chamberlain been tough in his negotiations with Hitler, he might have stopped the German leader from attacking Czechoslovakia since Hitler in March 1938 was not yet ready for war.

Negotiation is not a benefit conferred on a negotiating partner, but a tool to achieve an end. Whether to use the tool should depend on the prospects for success and alternatives, not moral judgments about the negotiating partner. In chapter 3, I argued that the United States should negotiate with Iran. This is not because I take a benign view of that regime—indeed a principal theme of this book is to criticize George W. Bush for having turned Iraq over to Iran—but because I don't see any good alternative for dealing with Iran's nuclear program. The Bush strategy of doing nothing is clearly not working and military action has potentially disastrous consequences.

As ambassador to Croatia during the Croatia and Bosnia wars, I negotiated frequently with evil men. Human rights advocates criticized our negotiating team for talking with war criminals, and some urged us to include civil society at the negotiating table. Indeed, I would have much preferred to deal

---

* In his January 2002 State of the Union speech, Bush compared Iraq, Iran, and North Korea to the World War II Berlin-Rome axis, calling the three countries an axis of evil. His speech was both geometrically and historically challenged. An axis runs between two points and not three (Japan was a nominal ally of Italy and Germany but not part of the Axis). And Germany and Italy were allies in the Second World War while, in 2002, Iran and Iraq were bitter enemies. Ironically, Bush's Iraq War resulted in a Tehran-Baghdad axis, as the two Shiite countries became close allies.

with the human-rights organizations and with civil society. After all, I shared their values, and we could have quickly reached agreement. But, to reach a peace agreement, we needed to negotiate with the men who had the guns. By negotiating with evil men, the United States achieved peace in Croatia and Bosnia. I have since seen some of my negotiating partners—when I testified in their war crimes trials!

Idealism and Pragmatism Are Compatible

The Dayton Peace Accords that formally ended the Bosnia War on November 21, 1995, followed massive U.S.-led NATO airstrikes on Bosnian Serb targets in August and September 1995. As U.S. peace negotiator Richard Holbrooke has written, the airstrikes and a simultaneous Croatian and Bosnian ground campaign inflicted enough damage on the war's architects that they were, at last, prepared to make peace. In retrospect, the U.S. intervention was a great success, but before it happened, it was very controversial. Both within the Clinton administration and outside, many argued that the United States had no vital interest in that part of the Balkans, and the suffering of the Bosnian people was insufficient justification for taking the risk of a prolonged involvement in a murky Balkan war. Others, myself included, argued strongly in favor of intervention. While we dressed up our arguments with a strategic rationale, the case for intervention was a moral one. At the end of the 20th century, we considered it intolerable that the United States should do nothing as civilians were deported from their homes in cattle cars, when men were starved in concentration camps, while artillery pounded undefended civilians in a European capital, and when men and boys were massacred by the thousands.

In the 1990s, Bosnia was not the only intervention that the United States made for moral or humanitarian reasons. In April 1991, President George H. W. Bush sent troops into northern Iraq to protect the Kurds from Saddam's retribution after a failed uprising (which he had encouraged), and in December 1992, he sent troops into Somalia to help deliver humanitarian assistance. And, in 1999, President Clinton fought an eighty-four-day air war against Serbia to prevent genocide against the Kosovo Albanians.

These interventions broke new ground. For the first time, the United States, along with others in the international community, were intervening in the internal affairs of a sovereign state where that state's government was unable or unwilling to protect its own citizens.

These interventions differed significantly from what George W. Bush has done in Iraq. Except for Kosovo, they were authorized or endorsed by the United Nations Security Council (and thirteen of the fifteen members supported the Kosovo intervention, which was not authorized because of a Russian veto). The United States led the interventions but had allies that provided significant military support and most of the funding. The peacekeeping missions that followed the Bosnia and Kosovo interventions were planned, professionally staffed, and adequately resourced. And, in all cases, U.S. goals were limited: to protect the Kurds, to feed Somalis, to end the Bosnia war, and to save the Kosovars. There was no thought that the United States should remake any of these countries into model democracies.*

---

* Some criticized the Dayton Accords for not recreating a unified multi-ethnic state, but we kept our focus on the narrower—and achievable—task of ending the war.

George W. Bush's ill-considered Iraq War may make Americans less likely to support these more narrow interventions that have saved hundreds of thousands of lives at a relatively low cost.

George W. Bush's many liberal critics often portray him as a shallow, self-centered man in the pocket of the special interests. At least in foreign affairs, I think this criticism is off the mark. I think Bush actually believes what he says about promoting democracy, eliminating tyranny, and not compromising with evil. Bush is an idealist, but he is not pragmatic. The combination of grand ambition with ignorance and weak leadership has, over the last eight years, done incalculable harm to U.S. national security. We are less secure than at any time since the Cold War and less liked and less effective than at any time in our modern history. The damage will not easily be repaired. But the greater damage will be if Bush's presidency is followed by a period of introspection and retrenchment in which manageable challenges go unaddressed. George W. Bush has given idealism a bad name, and this may be the greatest unintended consequence of all.

A Note on Sources

I have followed the Middle East professionally since I began work as a professional staff member for the Senate Foreign Relations Committee in 1979. Over the years, I have traveled extensively in the region and have developed close personal and professional ties with people in the region. This book is the product of those experiences.

I began working on Iraq at the start of the Iran-Iraq War in 1980 and first visited the country in 1984. In a subsequent visit in 1987, I came across the systematic destruction of Kurdish villages, and in 1988 I led a Foreign Relations Committee staff mission along the Iraq-Turkey border that interviewed survivors of Iraqi poison gas attacks on at least forty-eight Kurdish villagers in August 1988. At the invitation of Jalal Talabani, then a rebel leader and now Iraq's president, I went to Iraqi Kurdistan during the March 1991 uprising and was there when the Iraqi forces launched their counterattack. After the Kurdish safe-haven was established in April 1991, I made an additional six trips to rebel-held Kurdistan. In 2003, I was a consultant for

ABC News, arriving in Baghdad April 14, five days after U.S. forces toppled Saddam's statue in Firdos Square. During that trip, I traveled to the south as the Shiite religious parties began to consolidate their power, through Anbar as Saddam's forces began melting away, to Kirkuk and Mosul, and to Kurdistan. My experiences in Iraq are recounted in *The End of Iraq: How American Incompetence Created a War Without End.*

I left the U.S. government in November 2003 and since then have traveled to Iraq and surrounding countries every few months. These trips have provided material for articles that I have written about Iraq for the *New York Review of Books* and other publications. Some of my travel has been in connection with work on behalf of corporate clients, with several of which I have an ongoing business relationship.

I am also a regular traveler to Turkey, including to its Kurdish southeast. Many of these trips were in transit to Iraqi Kurdistan which, before Kurdistan opened its own airports in 2004, involved flying to Diyabakir (the main city in Turkey's southeast) and a four-hour road trip to the border. In 2002, while a professor at the National War College, I made a lengthy trip around Turkey, focused on the Kurdish question. And I regularly see Turkish journalists, politicians, diplomats, and academics in Istanbul and Ankara. Over the years, I have traveled frequently to the other countries discussed in this book—Pakistan, Syria, and Israel. While I have followed Iran closely and met with many Iranian opposition figures, I have never been to the country. In discussing nation building, I drew on my experiences in Croatia, Bosnia, and East Timor. From 1993 to 1998, I was the first U.S. Ambassador to Croatia, participating in the negotiations that ended the Bosnia and Croatia wars, and helping implement the subsequent peace agreements. In 2000 and 2001,

I was Director for Political, Constitutional and Electoral Affairs in the United Nations Transitional Administration in East Timor (UNTAET), one of the most ambitious nation-building efforts ever undertaken. For much of this period, I also served as the cabinet member for Political Affairs and Timor Sea in East Timor's first transitional government.

Although I have been both a scholar and a journalist, I am primarily a practitioner and, as such, not only write about ideas but also seek to implement them. In recent years, I have worked with my Kurdish friends to help them build an Iraqi Kurdistan that has a large measure of legal, political, and economic autonomy, a result I feel is not only just but will lead to greater stability. Although I continue to provide advice, I do not have any formal relationship with the Iraqi Kurds.* The views expressed in this book are mine alone.

In chapter 4, I make use of Aliza Marcus's *Blood and Belief: The PKK and the Kurdish Fight for Independence* (NYU Press, 2007). The book is an extraordinary feat of reporting, research, and writing that draws on extensive interviews with PKK members and defectors, including women guerrillas, and makes the reader feel as if he or she is inside the organization itself. In chapter 3, I make use of Trita Parsi's informative book *Treacherous Alliance—The Secret Dealings of Israel, Iran, and the United States* (Yale University Press, 2007), particularly for the 2003 Iranian non paper. In chapter 2, I refer to Douglas J. Feith's *War and Decision: Inside the Pentagon at the Dawn of the War on Terrorism* (Harper, 2008).

In writing this book, I have also made use of the daily

---

* Operating on a separate contract with him individually, a colleague at the Windham Resources Group does legal work for the KRG.

reporting in the *New York Times*, the *Washington Post*, the *Los Angeles Times*, the *Christian Science Monitor*, the *Boston Globe*, the *Kurdish Globe*, the *Guardian*, the *Turkish Daily News* and the *Star* (Beirut), among others. The most useful daily blog is Informed Comment, a summary of major articles in the international and Arab language press pulled together by University of Michigan Professor Juan Cole with his own analysis. I have also made use of articles, interviews, and reports on the websites of the United States Institute for Peace, the Council on Foreign Relations, the Brookings Institution, and the American Enterprise Institute. Speeches, congressional testimony, and transcripts can be found on the websites of the aforementioned institutions as well as those of the White House, the State Department, the Department of Defense, the Senate Foreign Relations Committee, and the House International Relations Committee.

Acknowledgments

This book is written as Americans are choosing a new president in an election campaign where Iraq and Iran are central issues. I wanted to write a book that might be relevant to that discussion and useful afterwards. This necessarily entailed a short production schedule.

Alice Mayhew, my editor at Simon & Schuster, made this happen. She worked her magic on the many phases of production so that the book would be timely. That included encouraging me, helping sharpen my arguments, and improving my prose. Roger Labrie, a collaborating editor on the project, contributed both to the substance of the book and enforced my several deadlines, and I am, in retrospect, grateful. Karen Thompson also helped. Gypsy da Silva, Associate Director of Copyediting, and Tom Pitoniak copy edited this book. Their many queries brought clarity, corrected mistakes, and suppressed extra words, for all of which the reader will be grateful. Rebecca Davis, in the publicity department, began lining up speeches and media appearances long before the book was ready and I am grateful to her and Victoria Meyer, the Director of Publicity. Michael Accordino designed the jacket. Thanks also to Irene Kheradi, Managing Editor, and to David Rosenthal, the publisher, who have assembled and maintained such an efficient and nice team of people.

I have been exceptionally fortunate to have Andrew Wylie as my agent, and not just for the obvious reason. He persuaded me to write my first book and encouraged this one. Although he represents many authors and has offices on several continents, Andrew operates as if I were his only client including answering emails and other queries in two minutes regardless of time of day.

Since 2004, Robert Silvers has made the pages of the *New York Review of Books* available for my writings on Iraq and Iran. Judging from the comments I get from all over the world, this is the publication to which policy makers not only subscribe but also read. While I have been working on this book, Bob has been understanding—although perhaps not entirely forgiving—of several missed deadlines for articles.

This book would not be possible without the insights of many friends in Iraq, Syria, Turkey, elsewhere in the Middle East and in Washington. Jalal Talabani, Masoud Barzani, Nechirvan Barzani, Kosrat Rasoul, Adnan Mufti, Fuad Husein, Barham Salih, Mohammad Ihssan, Hoshyer Zebari, Latif Rashid, Ahmad Chalabi, and Latif Rashid have been generous over the years with their time, in providing hospitality, and in seeing that the logistics are in place so that I could safely visit all parts of Iraq. Tony Touma provided his keen insight on Syria as well as making arrangements essential to my visits to that country. Cengiz Chandar is widely and rightly regarded as Turkey's most perceptive journalist and I am, when there, the beneficiary of his political and gastronomic insights. Osman Baydemir, the Mayor of Diyabakir, is not only a great host, but on one memorable occasion sent a snow plow to rescue me on the road out of his city. Steve and Nina Solarz are honorary Turks and visiting them in that country is the happy combination of education and relaxation in a place of incomparable beauty. Mark Siegel commutes between Islamabad and Washington and he and his wife Judy have educated me about both places. Bulent Aliriza generously offered to look over part of the manuscript. As always, I am grateful to Falah Bakir, Najmaldin Karim, and Kendal Nezan for their guidance and friendship.

None of the views expressed in this book should be attributed to anyone listed above. Several of my Iraqi friends would vigorously dissent from the main premises of the book while others might agree but would prefer I didn't say it. No one will agree with all that I have written. All errors of fact and interpretation are mine alone.

Benazir Bhutto was a close friend from the day when we started Harvard together in 1969. In December 2007, she was brutally murdered while trying, for a second time, to restore democracy to her beloved Pakistan. I miss her greatly but feel fortunate to have had the benefit over many years of her insights into her own country and its very volatile region.

I began to work professionally on the Middle East when I joined the staff of the Senate Foreign Relations Committee in 1979. For most of the fourteen years I worked for the Committee, Claiborne Pell was either the Ranking Minority Member or the Chairman. Daniel Patrick Moynihan served as Chairman of the Near East and South Asia subcommittee. Our country sorely misses their high principles and common sense. Many of the lessons cited in this book, I learned from them and from their extraordinary spouses, Nuala Pell and Liz Moynihan. They are also among the kindest and most loyal people I have known and this book is dedicated to the Pells and the Moynihans. It is a dedication shared with one to my wife, Tone Bringa, whose support and affection has been critical to this venture.

Index

About the Author

Peter W. Galbraith served as the first U.S. ambassador to Croatia. He is currently the Senior Diplomatic Fellow at the Center for Arms Control and Non-Proliferation and a contributor to the *New York Review of Books*. He is the author of *The End of Iraq*. He lives in Vermont.